Poverty, wealth and place in Britain, 1968 to 2005

Poverty, wealth and place in Britain, 1968 to 2005

Daniel Dorling, Jan Rigby, Ben Wheeler, Dimitris Ballas, Bethan Thomas, Eldin Fahmy, David Gordon and Ruth Lupton

JOSEPH ROWNTREE
FOUNDATION

First published in Great Britain in 2007 by

The Policy Press
Fourth Floor, Beacon House
Queen's Road
Bristol BS8 1QU
UK

Tel no   +44 (0)117 331 4054
Fax no   +44 (0)117 331 4093
Email   tpp-info@bristol.ac.uk
www.policypress.org.uk

Reprinted 2007

Published for the Joseph Rowntree Foundation by The Policy Press

ISBN 978 1 86134 995 8

British Library Cataloguing in Publication Data
A catalogue record for this book is available from the British Library.

Library of Congress Cataloging-in-Publication Data
A catalog record for this book has been requested.

Daniel Dorling, **Jan Rigby**, **Ben Wheeler**, **Dimitris Ballas** and **Bethan Thomas** are members of the Social and Spatial Inequalities research group in the Department of Geography, University of Sheffield. **Eldin Fahmy** and **David Gordon** are based in the University of Bristol School for Policy Studies, and in the Townsend Centre for International Poverty Research, where David is the Director. **Ruth Lupton** researches issues of poverty and place at the Institute of Education, University of London.

The **Joseph Rowntree Foundation** has supported this project as part of its programme of research and innovative development projects, which it hopes will be of value to policy makers, practitioners and service users. The facts presented and views expressed in this report are, however, those of the authors and not necessarily those of the Foundation.

The statements and opinions contained within this publication are solely those of the authors and not of the University of Bristol or The Policy Press. The University of Bristol and The Policy Press disclaim responsibility for any injury to persons or property resulting from any material published in this publication.

The Policy Press works to counter discrimination on grounds of gender, race, disability, age and sexuality.

Cover design by Qube Design Associates, Bristol
Front cover: photograph kindly supplied by www.third-avenue.co.uk
Printed in Great Britain by Latimer Trend, Plymouth

Contents

List of tables, figures and maps

Tables

Figures

Maps

Acknowledgements

We are grateful to the project advisory group for advice and constructive criticism throughout the development of the project. The group consisted of Jonathan Bradshaw, Glen Bramley, George Clark, Kate Green, Geoff Meen, Anne Power and Kirby Swales. Thanks are also due to Katharine Knox, who oversaw the project and chaired the advisory group on behalf of the project funders, the Joseph Rowntree Foundation. We acknowledge the assistance of Dan Vickers, who supplied maps for the original proposal; Mark Corver, who supplied data and helped with the analysis of higher education participation; and John Pritchard, for technical support throughout the project.

Data

Analyses use data from the UK Censuses of 1971, 1981, 1991 and 2001, which are Crown Copyright, the Family Expenditure Surveys and Poor Britain/Breadline Britain Surveys. Data were obtained via the Essex data archive and the Economic and Social Research Council (ESRC)/Joint Information Systems Committee (JISC) census programme. Geographical boundary data are subject to the following copyright statement: 'This work is based on data provided through EDINA UKBORDERS with the support of the ESRC and JISC and uses boundary material which is copyright of the Crown'.

Data produced by this project, including supplementary data such as a look-up table from census wards to tracts, and the tract cartogram used here, are available on the Social and Spatial Inequalities (SASI) website (www.sasi.group.shef.ac.uk/tracts).

Summary

Poverty and wealth

This report describes a project undertaken to assess the changing geographies of poverty and wealth in Britain over the past three decades of the 20th century, alongside additional material to bring the research up to the present day. Using established methodology – that used for the Breadline Britain indices – we constructed a coherent set of poverty measures for unchanging geographical areas for time periods around 1970, 1980, 1990 and 2000. For the same areas, we also constructed a number of novel measures of wealth.

These analyses allow us to divide the population of each area at each time period into five groups:

- *Core poor:* people who are income poor, materially deprived and subjectively poor.
- *Breadline poor:* people living below a relative poverty line, and as such excluded from participating in the norms of society.
- *Non-poor, non-wealthy:* the remainder of the population classified as neither poor nor wealthy.
- *Asset wealthy:* estimated using the relationship between housing wealth and the contemporary Inheritance Tax threshold.
- *Exclusive wealthy:* people with sufficient wealth to exclude themselves from the norms of society.

It should be noted that the core poor and exclusive wealthy households are subsets of the breadline poor and asset wealthy respectively (see F ure i below for an illustration of the distribution of all households in 2000).

Figure i: Distribution of all households (2000)

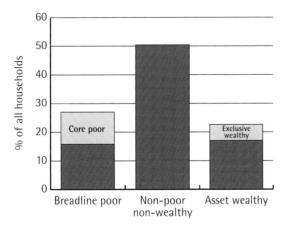

By producing these measures, we can observe the changing overall and geographical patterns of poverty and wealth over time. Since these calculations are largely dependent on decennial census data, we are currently unable to continue the time series beyond 2000/01. However, we have been able to investigate a variety of more recent data sources that have allowed us to infer the likely trends for the first decade of the new millennium.

Overall results up to 2000

The overall percentages of households in the core poor, breadline poor, asset wealthy and exclusive wealthy groups are shown in Figure ii below. The housing wealth data used for the asset wealthy measures shown here were not available for 1970, although figures were available for the middle of the 1990s, producing further insight into that decade.

Figure ii: Overall percentages of households in the core poor, breadline poor, asset wealthy and exclusive wealthy groups (1970-2000)

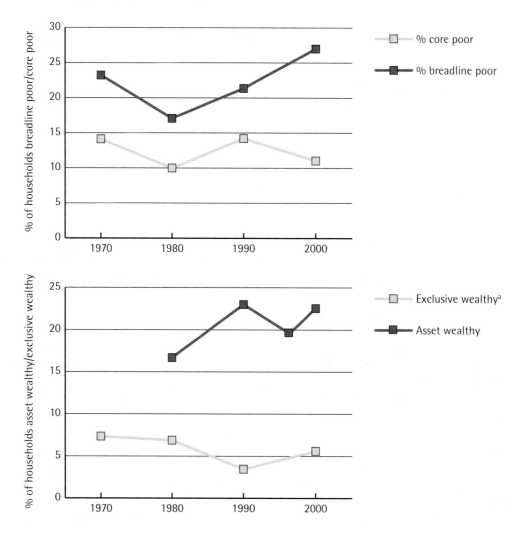

Note:[a] See Appendix 1 for variability around the exclusive wealth estimate and its trend.

Key points arising from the overall figures are:

• poverty and core poverty levels fell through the 1970s;
• they both then increased, returning by 1990 to similar levels to 1970;
• during the 1980s, while poverty levels were increasing, so were the proportions of asset wealthy households;
• exclusive wealthy households declined during the 1970s and 1980s, but increased during the 1990s;
• the 1990s saw a continuing rise in breadline poverty levels, but a concurrent decline in core poverty;
• during the early 1990s, the percentage of asset wealthy households fell, but recovered in the second half of the decade.

Spatial patterns and polarisation

In general, mapping of these poverty and wealth datasets indicate that wealth and poverty each demonstrate similar geographical patterns at every time period. The highest wealth and lowest poverty rates tend to be clustered in the South East of England (with the exception of most of Inner London); conversely the lowest wealth and highest poverty rates are concentrated in large cities and the industrialised/de-industrialising areas of Britain. The report reveals some interesting and substantial changes to this generalisation over time; however, there are issues in clearly identifying small pockets of rural and coastal wealth and poverty.

Analyses of the degree of polarisation and spatial concentration suggest that Britain's population became less polarised with regard to area breadline poverty rates during the 1970s. However, polarisation increased through the 1980s and the 1990s. Asset wealth also became more polarised during the 1980s, but this trend reversed in the first half of the 1990s, before polarisation could be seen to be increasing again at the end of that decade.

Since 2000

Our analyses of a variety of datasets covering the first five years of this decade have produced varying indications of changes in inequality since the turn of the millennium:

- Analysis of income data between 2003 and 2005 indicates that areas with the highest average incomes experienced the greatest increases, in both absolute and relative terms, while some areas with the lowest average incomes experienced declining incomes, increasing polarisation.
- The agenda for widening participation in higher education appears at a cursory level to have been working to some extent, with the greatest proportional increases in young people's participation rates occurring in areas with the lowest initial rates and highest poverty levels. However, other analyses have shown that this change in poorer areas can be explained by increases in participation in London, especially among minority ethnic groups, rather than among the poor in general. In absolute terms there is no narrowing of the education access gap.
- The change in the percentage of the working-age population claiming Jobseeker's Allowance (JSA) between 2000 and 2005 indicates that these years saw decreasing polarisation. Areas with the highest JSA claimant levels in 2000 tended to experience the greatest declines over the five years. This was even the case when the change was measured relatively.
- Asset wealth analysis indicates wealth between 1999 and 2003 to be rising most in areas in a band around 50-100 miles from London, and to be falling mostly in the cities of northern England, and across Scotland. Overall analysis suggests a trend for larger proportional increases in wealth in those areas with relatively low wealth levels, although absolute increases in the proportion of wealthy households were largest in areas with higher levels. The disproportionate trend, if it continues, should decrease polarisation, although at a very slow rate. Also, as the housing market is cyclical, equalising trends tend to be temporary.
- The proportion of working-age people claiming Incapacity Benefit (IB) between 2000 and 2005 increased in most areas of Britain. However, those areas with the very highest IB claimant rates and the highest poverty levels in 2000 tended to experience a fall in IB claimant rates. The time period coincides with the 'Pathways to Work' initiative, and our findings may reflect to a degree how such initiatives are spatially targeted, although the overall effects of such initiatives may be relatively limited (Fothergill and Wilson, 2006).

There is no clear single direction towards either increasing or decreasing polarisation among these five measures. Where there has been change, the magnitude of that change tends to be small, and so we should expect inequalities to increase or decrease slowly over time. Often closer analysis of what appear to be good news stories finds particular events have occurred related to the map of poverty that suggests that the trends may not be long term (particularly in relation to higher education and IB trends). All of our analyses of trends since 2000 suggest that there is no great reason to doubt the continuing validity of the picture presented when the 1999 Poverty and Social Exclusion Survey is combined with the 2001 Census: breadline poverty levels are rising and socioeconomic and geographical polarisation is increasing.

Conclusions

Since 1970, area rates of poverty and wealth in Britain have changed in significant ways. Over the past 15 years, more households have become poor, but fewer are very poor. Areas already wealthy have tended to become disproportionately wealthier, and we are seeing some evidence of increasing polarisation. In particular there are now areas in some of our cities where over half of all households are breadline poor.

Background

This report begins with a brief contextual discussion of the issues of poverty and wealth, especially with respect to their geographical aspects. Following from this, Chapters 2 and 3 describe the data and methods used to construct the measures of wealth and poverty (additional methodological detail is given in Appendix 1). Chapters 4 and 5 describe overall figures for Britain and geographical patterns of the various measures. Investigations of polarisation and spatial concentration are presented in Chapter 6 followed by consideration of more local issues in Chapter 7. The changing situation since the turn of the millennium is addressed in Chapter 8 using modern equivalents of Beveridge's five 'giant evils' as a framework to look at some of the key social issues of recent times. Finally, Chapters 9 and 10 discuss the problems and opportunities presented by this study, and the implications for the future of equality and inequality in Britain.

Poverty often refers to a lack of resources, and traditional poverty measures usually use low income or a lack of wealth as an indirect quantification of someone's inability to afford those resources. The approach used in this study is one of measuring directly what people cannot afford that most other people think are necessities in contemporary times (for example, a television, an annual holiday). Being rich is usually considered the opposite of being poor, but again it can be conceived of in different ways. Being wealth-rich and income-rich are different concepts; someone can be very wealthy, but have a very low income (for example, someone living in a stately home with much in the way of accumulated resources, but little cash income), and equally someone could have a high income and little wealth (for example, contractors with high levels of income but insufficient stability to buy their own homes or accumulate assets). However, the wealth-rich are less likely to be at risk of becoming poor than the income-rich. In Dixon and Margo's June 2006 publication *Population politics*, we are repeatedly reminded that one fifth of income-poor pensioners hold housing equity in excess of £100,000 per household. The background to these concepts with regard to this study is discussed further below.

A history of the geography of poverty

There is a long history of studying the geography of poverty in Britain, although every so often the importance of that geography is rediscovered (Philo, 1995). In contrast the geography of wealth is rarely seen in work on Britain, although occasionally the locations of those featuring in 'Who's Who' are mapped – or the *Sunday Times* Rich List remarked on. In this report previously developed methodology is reapplied to produce a consistent data series of the levels of poverty by area in Britain for two types of poverty, and a new methodology introduced to produce comparable area estimates for the wealthy.

In 1901 Seebohm Rowntree published *Poverty: A study of town life*, which was one of the very first detailed surveys at such a fine geographical scale. His book included a map of York shaded by population characteristics (Rowntree, 2000). He identified two areas of contiguous streets as the poorest districts. The smaller area lay on the western bank of the river, within the old city walls, centred on Micklegate. The larger area, east of the city, centred on Walmgate to the south. A century later, the first maps are being drawn of the entire country to a similar level of detail that Rowntree observed. The new maps (Vickers, 2005) show how the poorest areas of York now lie largely outside the city walls. However, there are now over two dozen 'poorest' areas within the new boundaries of York. Many appear in outlying suburbs, one within the model urban village of New Earswick.

The new 'poorest' areas are not far from the old. To the west, just outside of Micklegate, are new pockets of poverty in once well-to-do streets. To the east, where there were fields in 1901 outside Walmgate, one of the largest areas of poverty can now be found. However, poverty is also now found scattered across the city, often within areas now described as 'typical' between which are the 'comfortable suburban estates' of 2001. When the maps are compared what is most similar is the rarity with which a 'comfortable estate' abuts an area of 'constrained circumstances'.

There are two other major changes to the social geography of York. Firstly, most of the city centre and the new campus of the University of York are now labelled as 'melting pot' areas characterised by young single people. This is where in 1901 Rowntree drew a circle to highlight the concentration of licensed premises and clubs in the city centre. The second change is by far the most significant. Whereas in 1901 only a few streets were affluent and these were some of the major thoroughfares, now the majority of the land within the new city boundaries is made up of comfortable estates and, where they come to an end they abut a blue sea on the 2001 map labelled 'idyllic countryside'. Whereas the map of 1901 can be read as highlighting affluence in the midst of poverty, the map one century on is of poverty in the midst of affluence.

This is a necessarily brief look at the history of poverty research; even the geographically related research literature is vast, and far from concentrated on Britain.

Recent poverty research

At the turn of the century, much work was published updating our understanding of poverty geography in Britain (Gregory et al, 2000). However, our understanding of the changing geography of poverty in the UK is hampered by a lack of consistent poverty measures. We do not measure income directly in the census, and we do not have an agreed poverty line as in the US (although this is not necessarily a bad thing, given that the level of the US poverty line is often criticised for being set very low). Measures such as benefit claims and indices of deprivation have been used, as well as individual census variables, but these have not been held constant over time or spatial units.

The Breadline Britain method, on which the latest report was published in January 2006 (Pantazis et al, 2006), measured relative poverty based on a lack of the perceived necessities of life. This has been widely accepted as a good measure of relative poverty. These surveys, the Breadline Britain Surveys, showed that: 'in 1983 14% of households lacked three or more necessities because they could not afford them. That proportion had increased to 21% in 1990 and to over 24% by 1999. (Items defined as necessities are those that more than 50% of the population believes "all adults should be able to afford and which they should not have to do without")' (Gordon et al, 2000). This approach is ideal for application to this project, as it can be replicated for a time series where we have a census and poverty survey occurring at roughly the same time, which has been the case for approximately every 10 years since 1970. Alternative approaches are not useful here; for example the Index of Multiple Deprivation and its predecessors are not comparable over time. More simplistic, individually focused indicators of poverty that can be more headline grabbing (see, for example, Winnett, 2006) are not good measures of poverty or the impacts of social policy changes.

Findings of poverty research are equivocal. In 2003 it was thought that the government was on target to reduce child poverty by a million (Sutherland et al, 2003). However, by 2006 it became evident that this had not been achieved (Brewer et al, 2006a). Research for the Joseph Rowntree Foundation (JRF) found that in order to meet the target of ending child poverty by 2020, the government would have to add around £28 billion to planned annual spending, and that this target is unlikely to be met under current policies (Evans and Scarborough, 2006; Hirsch, 2006). Contrary to the fall in poverty as measured by income, poverty as measured by expenditure was found to be rising (Dixon and Margo, 2006; Palmer et al, 2006).

Further work for JRF confirmed that while poverty based on income had fallen from 25% to 22% between 1996/97 and 2002/03, an alternative measure based on expenditure found poverty to have risen from 20% to 22% over the same time period (Brewer et al, 2006b). Further, the poorest groups in society are also the most likely to be financially excluded and run into debt problems that may be caused and exacerbated by 'home-collecting industry' money-lending practices (Leyshon et al, 2006).

Qualitative studies of poor neighbourhoods over the same period (for example, Lupton, 2003, 2005) show a similarly mixed picture, with falling worklessness and increased benefits raising the incomes of working families, but little impact on the relative position of neighbourhoods and continuing problems of debt and in-work poverty. In the context of this overall picture, there were variations between neighbourhoods and ethnic groups.

Wealth and affluence

While there is a considerable body of work on poverty, including a wide range of approaches that attempt to measure poverty, this is not matched by the amount of literature that addresses wealth. Indeed, it is remarkable how little literature there is on the subject. Attempts to measure wealth at a sub-national level do exist, but the assessment of the amount of wealth of individuals or households at the higher levels is compromised by the ways in which such wealth can be 'hidden', for example in asset ownership by companies rather than individuals, and in complex overseas financial management. Indeed, 'wealth management' is a service that is inherently denied to most people. However, in recent times there has been an upsurge in popular interest in the most wealthy and those earning the most income, fuelled by media publications such as the *Sunday Times* Rich List (and the US Forbes equivalent), and explored in depth in publications such as Lansley's *Rich Britain* (2006). Wealth inequality is a concept that is much more prevalent in the UK and US than most other affluent countries.

In 2004, the Institute for Public Policy Research (IPPR) produced an assessment of *The state of the nation* (Paxton and Dixon, 2004) with regard to social justice in Britain. They concluded that while '...Britain is a fairer, better place in 2004 than it was in 1994, it remains far from socially just' (p 60). Among other observations, the report found that wealth distribution had continued to become more unequal during the 1990s. A further report from the IPPR found that the decade 1991-2001 saw the wealthiest tenth of the population increase their wealth holdings from 47% to 56% of total wealth (IPPR, 2004), while the 'rise and rise of the new super-wealthy' in Britain has been described and analysed in great detail recently by Lansley (2006). As will be seen below, these findings are largely in accordance with the research presented here.

There is a substantial body of work exploring income inequality, and in the UK this inequality has remained at obstinately high levels. From the late 1970s to the mid-1990s, income inequality grew at a faster rate in the UK than even within the US. The distribution of wealth demonstrates much greater inequality than income, but has not followed the same path (Lansley, 2006). The gap fell throughout the 20th century, until the late 1980s, but then began widening in the early 1990s. Detailed data are only available for the top 1% of the wealthy in the UK, but show that their share of total personal wealth grew from 17% in 1988 to 23% in 2002 (Tulip, 2002). At the other end, the share of the bottom 50% dropped from 10% in 1986 to 6% in 2002. Britain is moving back towards levels of wealth inequality last experienced more than 30 years ago and this is considered to be an under-estimate of the true extent of inequality (Lansley, 2006).

The most recent UK statistics released do contradict this finding to some extent; Table 1 presents National Statistics from 2006 that indicate very slight reductions in both wealth (2002-03) and income (2003/04-2004/05) inequalities (National Statistics, 2006a, 2006b). The wealth data used for the National Statistics are subject to fairly substantial annual fluctuation, since they are based on wills and hence can be influenced by the deaths of a small number of very wealthy people.

Table 1: Trends in the distribution of marketable wealth (assets owned that could be sold, that is, excluding occupational pensions that cannot be 'cashed in')

| | % of total personal wealth owned by | | |
	Top 1%	Top 5%	Bottom 50%
1923	61	82	0
1938	55	77	0
1950	47	74	0
1960	34	59	0
1970	30	54	0
1976	21	38	8
1986	18	36	10
1991	17	35	8
1996	20	40	7
1999	23	43	6
2002	24	45	6
2003	21	40	7

Source: Adapted from Lansley (2006, p 235) and National Statistics (2006a); zeros were in original table

In the UK the rich largely operate in the private sector and remain largely privileged by upbringing (not necessarily just by financial inheritance). Lansley suggests they are now perhaps more obsessed with money than social status, they enjoy power, exercising it in different ways in terms of lavish living and celebrity status, some influence political processes, and some accept social responsibilities, but the modern equivalents to the philanthropists such as Lever, Cadbury and Rowntree are not readily found.

We have noted that one of the major characteristics of wealth is the power to 'go private', but this process clearly impacts on others who have to manage within what remains, for example, state education or health or housing provision. In terms of opportunities, it has been observed that less able richer children overtake more able poorer children by the age of five (*The Independent*, November 2003, quoted in Lansley, 2006, p 202). But what do you have to have, or be able to do, to be wealthy?

Scott (1994) uses a framework of citizenship to define wealth. This follows Townsend's approach to poverty as relative deprivation (Townsend, 1979), with the poor lacking the opportunities to enjoy a standard of living commensurate with societal norms, and by extension that they are 'deprived of the resources that would allow them to participate as a full citizen of their society' (Scott, 1994, p 150). From this, as people are deprived, so others may be privileged. Here privilege is interpreted as a 'private benefit unavailable to the public' (p 151), which the privileged can then enjoy, and which the public, particularly the deprived, are excluded from. Hence deprivation and privilege are complementary, but Scott acknowledges that the former is much easier to determine. He observes the delineation by poverty lines (below which are the deprived) and wealth lines (above which are the privileged), the line being the point at which exclusion takes place. Hence the wealth line 'marks a point in the distribution of resources at which the possibility of enjoying special benefits and advantages of a private sort escalates disproportionately to any increase in resources' (p 152). Essentially, while the poor are deprived from roles of citizenship, the wealthy are able to choose to participate less in the public context.

Rentoul (1987) uses Townsend's approach to suggest that the 'wealth line' can be positioned based on the amount of money needed to eliminate poverty, thus we need to estimate the point 'in the distribution of resources above which this could be made available' (Scott, 1994, p 155). A similar method has been employed in a recent study conducted at the United Nations Development Programme (UNDP) (Medeiros, 2006). Updating Mack and Lansley's 1985 study, Rentoul (1987) calculated that £12 billion per annum is needed to remove the deprivation of 10 million people. To raise this would entail setting an income ceiling at £22,000 (possibly from £16,400 salary plus interest on £110,000 assets). This figure is thought to correspond with Schifferes' study (1986) where people believed that those with an income over £20,000 and assets over £100,000 would be rich, which corresponded to 2% of the adult population.

Researching the wealth of the US, Wolff (1998) suggests that, moving beyond income, wealth contributes towards well-being. He argues that wealth in the form of assets can be realised to facilitate consumption, that the release of these assets can provide support in terms of socioeconomic crisis, such as unemployment or family breakdown, and wealth is also associated with issues of power in terms of representation and governance. For individuals and households, wealth often has a temporal dimension, increasing at the later stages of a life course when mortgages have been paid, and children become independent. It might therefore have a more predictable trajectory than poverty.

Wolff (1998) studied household wealth inequality in the US, based on the Federal Reserve Board's Surveys of Consumer Finances in 1983, 1989, 1992 and 1995. A high-income supplement to the study provides over-sampling of the most wealthy. Wolff uses two measures of wealth:

- *Net worth (marketable wealth)* calculated as the difference between total assets and total liabilities. Total assets comprise the gross value of owner-occupied housing and other property, savings, stocks and securities, the surrender values of pension and life insurance plans, net equity in unincorporated businesses and equity in trust funds. Liabilities comprise mostly mortgage and other consumer debt.
- *Financial wealth*, which is net worth minus net equity in owner-occupied housing reflecting the fact that this is often very difficult to liquidate at short notice.

The results show the distribution of wealth (Table 2).

Wolff noted that the median household wealth dropped 10% between 1983 and 1995, but that mean net worth rose 2.9%, indicating high-end growth. The largest gains in absolute and relative wealth were made by the top 1% of the wealthiest. In 1995, the profile of the top 1% was that they were almost twice as likely to be in the 45-74 age group as the total population, four times as likely to have attended graduate school, almost twice as likely

Table 2: The distribution of wealth from Wolff's study of the US (1998), 1983–95

	% share of net worth			
	Top 1%	**Next 4%**	**Top 20%**	**Bottom 40%**
1983	33.8	22.3	81.3	0.9
1989	37.4	21.6	83.5	−0.7
1992	37.2	22.8	83.8	0.4
1995	38.5	21.8	83.9	0.2

to have self-reported excellent health status, more than four times as likely to be self-employed, and 95% were white compared with 78% of the overall population of the US.

In the US, owner-occupied housing was the largest single important asset, accounting for 30% of total assets. This proportion proved consistent over time, although for the richest 1%, housing only accounted for 6% of their wealth, the majority being financial stocks and securities. In contrast, almost two thirds of the wealth of the bottom 80% was invested in their own homes, leaving them with very little resistance to financial shocks such as unemployment.

In Britain, there is an unexplored geographical dimension to the implications of owner-occupied housing being the main wealth asset: particularly for those who retire, wealth might become even more dependent on where they live. For example, a coastal property in South West England will have accumulated considerable value, which could be realised to perhaps pay for care in the later stages of life. A similar retirement to a remote part of Scotland may have seen a comparable decrease in wealth over the past 20 years, rendering the same quality of care unachievable. Housing wealth is a key form of wealth. As will be seen in Chapter 3, it makes up a significant amount of total household wealth and therefore it is particularly important when determining the degree to which a household is asset wealthy or exclusive wealthy.

2

Methods

Time periods and data sources

The main analysis here has involved calculating the number of households in each of the four categories (described below) – core poor, breadline poor, asset wealthy and exclusive wealthy – for each area of Britain, for each of four time periods. The survey and census data determine the exact years under consideration, and these are detailed in Table 3 below. However, for clarity and simplicity, we refer to these time periods as 1970, 1980, 1990 and 2000, and to the changes over each decade – the 1970s, 1980s and 1990s. Data on housing wealth were available for additional periods between census years, and the data for 1996 have been used in order to gain insight into the changes during the 1990s in more detail, since economic circumstances in Britain changed substantially around the middle of this decade.

Table 3: Time periods and datasets

Study year	Census year	Poverty Survey year	Housing wealth data year	Family Expenditure Survey years
1970	1971	1968	n/a	1970-72 (3 years)
1980	1981	1983	1983	1980-81 (2 years)
1990	1991	1990[a]	1990	1990-92 (3 years)
(1996)	n/a	n/a	1996	n/a
2000	2001	1999[a]	1999	1999/2000 and 2000/01 (2 years)

Note: [a] The analysis of the 1990 and 1999 Poverty Surveys to produce small area poverty measures (the Breadline Britain indices) had been completed as part of previous JRF projects.
Source: Gordon and Pantazis (1997); Gordon et al (2000)

The next full decade for consideration in this series would be 2001-11 (census years), and this will not be possible until detailed data are released from the 2011 Census, most likely around 2013. Therefore, the years since 2000 have been considered separately from this series, and are described following discussion of the main analysis below. While this post-2000 time period is not directly comparable with those previous decades, our additional analysis gives an indication of the likely direction of changes in some aspects of the geography of wealth and poverty over the first decade of the new millennium, and can be viewed in the context of other more recent work described in 'Recent poverty research' (page 2) above.

One decision to be made with a study such as this is the unit of analysis – the choice is usually whether to analyse households or people. Our reason for using households is largely pragmatic. In combining the census and the surveys, the most appropriate unit is the household, since that is the sampling unit (for the surveys). It is also the appropriate level for information such as tenure or car ownership. Household size and composition tends to vary with socioeconomic status, but potential bias is controlled in the breadline method by adjusting household income for these factors. Given that our wealth analysis relies on housing equity, the household is again the most appropriate unit.

Geography

The geographical areas used here are 'tracts', which have been specifically designed to allow comparison of social statistics over time (SASI, 2006). Each tract approximates half of a parliamentary constituency, resulting in Britain being divided into 1,282 areas, each of roughly equivalent population. These areas remain constant over time, and for each time period, a look-up table is available to aggregate data for census wards and similar small areas into the tracts (see www.sasi.group.shef.ac.uk/tracts).

The mean population of a tract in 2001 was around 45,000 people, with some variation leading to a minimum of 12,000 and a maximum of 90,000. Where possible, tracts have been aligned with local authority areas – for example, the London Borough of Barking and Dagenham is coterminous with four constituent tracts, Dagenham East and West, and Barking North and South. In more rural areas, constituencies have occasionally been divided into an 'urban' tract and a 'rural' tract, for example, the 'Shrewsbury and Atcham' constituency is divided into Shrewsbury and the surrounding more rural parts of North Shropshire.

3

The measures: breadline poor, core poor, asset wealthy and exclusive wealthy

Where possible, for each time period, four distinct groups of households are identified for each tract:

1. *Core poor:* defined theoretically according to Bradshaw's (1972a, 1972b, 1994) Taxonomy of Need as people suffering from a combination of Normative, Felt, and Comparative poverty, that is, people who are simultaneously income poor, necessities/ deprivation poor and subjectively poor (see Bradshaw and Finch, 2003).

2. *Breadline poor:* under the Relative Poverty Line, defined theoretically by Townsend (1979) as the resource level that is so low that people are excluded from participating in the norms of society, and measured by the Breadline Britain Index (see Gordon and Pantazis, 1997 and Gordon et al, 2000 for a detailed discussion of how the Index is derived). This is the same theoretical definition of poverty used by the European Union to measure poverty and social exclusion.

3. *Asset wealthy:* those living above an asset wealth line. Here, we use housing wealth data (developed for a previous project, reported in Thomas and Dorling, 2004) to estimate the number of wealthy households as those living above an asset wealth threshold, for time periods comparable to those used for the poverty measures. While housing wealth is a particular facet of wealth, it is most likely correlated with more general wealth (including 'income wealth'). Given that this method uses explicitly geographical wealth data, it is potentially more geographically accurate than the exclusive wealth method that uses geographical census data to estimate the spatial distribution of wealth from proxy characteristics of the wealthy classified using non-geographical survey data. Since the census is also better suited to recording traits associated with poverty than wealth, it is useful to also calculate a measure that does not rely on census data.

4. *Exclusive wealthy:* those living above a (higher) wealth line, defined following the discussion of Scott (1994); a resource level that is so high that people are able to exclude themselves from participating in the norms of society (if they so wish). No one to our knowledge has tried to operationalise a wealth line such as this, but this can be done using Family Expenditure Survey data in combination with the Households Below Average Income (HBAI) adjustments to the incomes of the very 'rich'. The HBAI adjustments account for household size and type when considering household income, and are the same as those used in the Breadline Britain methodology. The adjusted Family Expenditure Survey data can then be used to discover the average band/level of income at which children go to independent schools, people use private healthcare, have second homes, boats, pay private club membership fees, etc. Two methods are described below for estimating the geographical distribution of exclusive wealthy

households, one using the census, and one using the housing data used to estimate asset wealth.

It is assumed that the core poor are a subset of the breadline poor, and similarly that the exclusive wealthy are a subset of the asset wealthy.

By defining these four groups of households, we also define a fifth 'middle' group by default – those that are neither poor nor wealthy, counted as the remainder of households in a tract after accounting for groups 2 and 3 (which are presumed to contain groups 1 and 4, respectively). As described above, the availability of the data determine the exact time periods under consideration, and in the case of housing wealth data, we do not have data for 1970 or any time around then, limiting the time series with respect to this wealth measure.

Poverty

The methodology used to estimate the number of breadline poor households for each area for each time period is well established and has been used previously for similar research, as described above. This approach is increasingly being used elsewhere for poverty measurement, for example by the Department for Work and Pensions (DWP, 2002). For our study, the method is extended to earlier poverty surveys and censuses to create a consistent time series across the three decades. The methods used with the 1990 and 1999 Poverty Surveys have been described in detail previously (Gordon and Pantazis, 1997; Gordon et al, 2000). The methods developed here for the 1968 and 1983 Surveys are very similar, and are described in Appendix 1.

In essence, the method uses the information from a detailed poverty survey, carried out on a sample of 1,000 or 2,000 households, to classify each household in the survey as 'poor' or 'not poor'. The survey also includes information comparable to that collected by the census, such as household composition, tenure, car ownership and social class. The survey data can then be analysed to assess the relationship between these census-type variables and the poor/not poor classification of households in the survey. These relationships are applied to census data to estimate the number of poor households in each area for which census data is available. For example, the analysis of the 1999 Poverty and Social Exclusion Survey indicated that the total number of breadline poor households was equal to the following:

57.6% of overcrowded households (more than one person per room) +
35.7% of households renting from local authorities or housing associations +
32.4% of lone-parent households +
30.3% of households with an unemployed Household Reference Person (HRP) +
18.4% of households with no car +
16.5% of households renting from private landlords +
16.1% of households with a member with a limiting long-term illness +
13.5% of households with no central heating or without sole use of amenities +
11.3% of households with HRP in a low social class (National Statistics Socioeconomic Classification [NS-SEC] 6, 7 or 8).

A simple hypothetical example may be useful here for clarification. Assume that, according to the census, there are 100 households in a particular area, of which:

5 are classified as 'overcrowded'
15 are renting from local authorities or housing associations

10 are 'lone-parent households'
10 have an unemployed HRP
30 households have no car
50 households rent from private landlords
10 households have someone with a limiting long-term illness
5 households have no central heating or are without the sole use of amenities
40 households have their HRP in a low social class.

In order to estimate the breadline poor households in this area we would need to apply the respective weightings described above to the total number of households in each category. For instance, it would be assumed that of the five households that live in overcrowded conditions 57.6% would be breadline poor (that is, 2.88 households). Likewise, of the 15 households renting from local authorities or housing associations, 35.7% would be assumed to be breadline poor (5.35 households). Applying the breadline poor weightings to each household category total would give us an estimate of the total number of breadline poor households in the area, which in the context of this example would be 35 households. Table 4 illustrates how this calculation would be carried out.

Table 4: An example of estimating breadline poor in a hypothetical census area

Estimating breadline poor households	Breadline poor weightings (%)	Census totals	Estimating breadline poor in the area (column B x column C)
A	B	C	D
Overcrowded households (more than one person per room)	57.6	5	2.88
Households renting from local authorities or housing associations	35.7	15	5.35
Lone-parent households	32.4	10	3.24
Households with an unemployed HRP	30.3	10	3.03
Households with no car	18.4	30	5.52
Households renting from private landlords	16.5	50	8.25
Households with a member with a limiting long-term illness	16.1	10	1.61
Households with no central heating or without sole use of amenities	13.5	5	0.67
Households with HRP in a low social class (NS-SEC 6, 7 or 8)	11.3	40	4.52
Estimated number of breadline poor households in the area			35

The 2001 Census tells us the number of households in each area with these characteristics, so the percentages can be applied and result in an estimate of the number of poor households in each census area.[1]

The core poor method developed for this study is an extension of the breadline method. The concept of core poverty is used here to describe those households that are simultaneously income poor, deprivation poor and subjectively poor. The analyses outlined here use the following definitions of these terms, using the 1983 Poverty Survey as an example (core poor definitions for other decades used the same methods, with precise definitions as appropriate to the specific survey).

---

[1] Census weightings for breadline poor and core poor households at each time period are given in Appendix 1.

Income poverty: equivilised (that is, after housing costs) net weekly household income less than 70%[2] of equivilised net weekly household income of all sampled households.

Deprivation poor: following Whelan et al (2001), deprivation is operationalised here by the Basic Deprivation Index in which a household is said to be poor if they respond positively to any of the following statements:

- In arrears on rent/mortgage, utilities and hire purchase payments
- Buy second-hand not new clothes
- Cannot afford meat, chicken or fish every second day
- Cannot afford to keep home adequately warm
- Cannot afford carpets in living areas (Whelan et al, 2001 use inability to afford to replace worn out furniture; this variable is not available in the 1983 Poverty Survey)
- Cannot afford a week's annual holiday away from home
- Cannot afford to have friends/family for a meal once a month

Subjectively poor: the respondent was asked the following question about their household circumstances: 'Do you think you could *genuinely* say you are poor now?' (Question 23). Respondents who answered positively (that is, 'all the time' or 'sometimes') are considered to be subjectively poor.

Households (in the 1983 Survey) are therefore defined as core poor if their equivilised household income is less than 70% of the median *and* they are deprivation poor (according to the basic deprivation measure) *and* they consider their household to be poor 'sometimes' or 'all the time'.

The poverty rates using the Breadline Britain methodology are well-recognised indicators, modelled with explicit reference to reliability and validity. However, they are still subject to some potential biases, particularly with regard to monitoring change over time. One criticism of the method is that the general standard of living has risen so much over the 30 years to 2000, that luxury items seem more 'normal', but a larger proportion of the population lack them than lacked 'essential' items in the past. People in recent times who actually lack the 'luxury' items perceived as normal may not feel deprived with respect to those items. This argument tends to fail with time. When Seebohm Rowntree wrote in 1901 that the poor should be able to afford a stamp to post a letter there were some who thought this frivolous. None would argue so today. Those items we argue over as being essential or non-essential today are almost always seen as essential tomorrow, even if they were unheard of yesterday.

Wealth

The asset wealth method uses tract-level data on housing wealth sourced from previous research by the authors (Thomas and Dorling, 2004). For each year, for each tract,[3] we have information on average house price by type of dwelling, and similarly the number of homes that are owned outright and being bought (with a mortgage) by type of

---

[2]   Note that the 70% threshold that we use here is also the Department for Work and Pensions' new material deprivation and relative low income child poverty measure (see DWP, 2003 and Rio Expert Group on Poverty Statistics, 2006).

[3]   Housing wealth data were unavailable for Scotland for 1999, so values for Scottish tracts in this year were interpolated from 1996 and 2002 data.

dwelling. Using these data, for each tract we estimate the distribution of housing wealth, and subsequently the number of households with housing wealth exceeding a threshold considered to make that household wealthy.[4] While the notion of what counts as 'wealthy' is slightly vague, and therefore contentious, we use the contemporary Inheritance Tax threshold as an indicator of asset wealth. Hence a household with sufficient total wealth for its estate to be liable to Inheritance Tax is considered wealthy.

Since people hold wealth in forms additional to their housing, it is not appropriate to simply apply the Inheritance Tax threshold to our estimated distribution of housing wealth across the population of a tract. Instead, we consider for each time period the proportion of national wealth held in housing,[5] and apply this proportion to the Inheritance Tax threshold, as listed in Table 5. For example, the Inheritance Tax threshold in 1999 was £231,000. At this time, 33.2% of wealth was held in housing, so we use a housing wealth (that is, positive equity) threshold of £76,692 (33.2% of £231,000) to define the asset wealthy. So, for example, a household with an estimated housing wealth of £80,000 in this year is assumed to have other assets adding up to this wealth, which are sufficient such that that the total household wealth would well exceed the £231,000 threshold and therefore would be liable to Inheritance Tax.

The assumptions made here mean that our overall assessment of the proportion of households considered to be wealthy must be viewed in the light of our definition. However, these assumptions are unlikely to strongly influence the relative levels of wealth calculated for different parts of the country, and hence the geographical patterns we observe should be reliable. Some validation of the observed geographical patterns is possible using alternative datasets associated with wealth (see Appendix 1).

Table 5: Inheritance Tax thresholds and proportions of wealth held in housing used to derive asset wealth thresholds

Year	Inheritance Tax Threshold (£)[a]	Housing wealth as a percentage of total wealth (%)	Housing wealth threshold (£)
1983	60,000	31.7	19,020
1990	118,000	40.3	47,554
1996	200,000	29.8	59,600
1999	231,000	33.2	76,692

Note: [a] Inheritance Tax was only introduced in 1986/87. The 1983 figure is the threshold for its predecessor, Capital Transfer Tax.
Source: Institute for Fiscal Studies, 'Fiscal facts', www.ifs.org.uk/ff/iht.xls

Although differing in theoretical definition, in practice the exclusive wealth measure was calculated using a similar method as for asset wealth, but using a higher housing wealth threshold to locate the exclusive wealthy. Family Expenditure Survey data were analysed to estimate the proportion of households found nationally with sufficient income/expenditure to exclude themselves from the norms of society, as defined at the start of this Chapter.[6] According to our analysis, in 1971, 7.4% of all households (at national level) were exclusive

---

[4] Further details of the method are given in Appendix 1.

[5] Based on data from Thomas and Dorling (2004, p 10).

[6] These households typically have extremely high expenditure on goods and services such as private healthcare, private school fees, private domestic services and so on (see Appendix 1 for more details).

wealthy. The exclusive wealthy household rates for 1981, 1991 and 2001 were 6.9%, 3.5% and 5.6% respectively. The Family Expenditure Survey analysis is described in detail in Appendix 1.

We used the Family Expenditure Survey-derived exclusive wealthy proportion at each time period to calibrate the asset wealth model threshold, in order to produce an estimate of the number of exclusive wealthy households in each tract. This calibration process adjusted the housing wealth threshold until it generated a national total proportion equal to that in the contemporary Family Expenditure Survey data. For instance, as noted above, in 2001 5.6% of all households nationally were exclusive wealthy. In order to estimate the geographical distribution of these households across tracts we developed and implemented a method that determined the threshold required in order to select the wealthiest households making up 5.6% of all households nationwide.

Again, a simple example may be useful here for clarification. Let us assume that we have a hypothetical country with 30 households living in five tracts. Table 6 illustrates this hypothetical situation and lists all households in every tract (row) in ascending order of housing equity.

Table 6: An example of estimating exclusive wealthy households

Tract	Housing equity (£)							Total number of households in the tract
1	5,000	5,500	8,000	10,000	12,000	13,000		6
2	3,000	6,000	10,000	12,000	15,000	**20,000**		6
3	3,000	7,000	12,000	15,000	**16,000**			5
4	4,500	5,500	6,000	8,000	10,000	12,000		6
5	3,000	5,000	5,500	6,000	7,000	8,000	8,500	7

So, the first household in hypothetical tract 1 has an estimated housing equity of £5,000, which is the lowest in this track. The second household has a housing equity of £5,500, whereas the sixth household in the row has the highest equity in the tract (£13,000). Likewise, in tract 2, the first household has an equity of £3,000, the second household an equity of £6,000 etc. Of the total 30 hypothetical households in all tracts the household with the highest equity resides in tract 2 and has an equity of £20,000. As noted above, according to the analysis of the Family Expenditure Survey data 6.9% of all households in 1971 at national level were exclusive wealthy. If we were to apply this rate in the context of example shown in Table 5 then of the 30 households there would be approximately two exclusive wealthy households (6.7% of the 30 households). The wealthiest two households in Table 1 reside in tract 2 and tract 3 (with a housing equity of £20,000 and £16,000 respectively). This example demonstrates a simplified version of the approach adopted to estimate the geographical distribution of exclusive wealthy households, by implementing the national rates across all tracts. It should be noted that having to apply this method to all tracts using the real data involved the consideration of a large number of different thresholds to locate the wealthiest households across all tracts, in order to identify the best combination that would result in them adding up to the national percentage in each year.

The housing wealth thresholds that resulted from harmonising the asset wealth method with the Family Expenditure Survey-derived exclusive wealth total are presented in

Table 7. This method produces plausible data and geographies, described in the results sections below.

Table 7: Housing wealth thresholds used to define exclusive wealthy households using the asset wealthy method

Year	Exclusive wealth threshold (£)
1983	33,250
1990	136,000
1996[a]	127,000
1999	182,000

Note: [a] The exclusive wealthy proportion for 1996 was not available. Therefore, the mean of the values for 2000 and 1990 was used to derive the threshold.

The second exclusive wealth measure for tracts was calculated using the same Family Expenditure Survey analysis combined with contemporary census data in a similar manner to the breadline poor measures. The estimates produced using this method were not considered reliable, largely due to the inability of data from the census to effectively differentiate the very wealthy. This alternative method and its results are discussed in Appendix 1.

One issue with the measures of wealthy households based on housing wealth is that they are likely to be influenced by the state of the housing market; changes observed, especially in southern England during the early 1990s, are likely to be influenced by the housing market crash. It is therefore possible that relying on housing to track the assets of the wealthy is less reliable at this time. However, since housing forms a major component of most people's wealth, the crash is likely to have had a very real effect on the wealth of people at that time, even if it was only a temporary effect. Another issue with these indicators is the application of the national proportion of wealth held in housing to every tract. It is possible – perhaps likely – that there is regional and local variation in this proportion, which might lead to the nationally adjusted Inheritance Tax based wealth threshold being inappropriate. However, in the absence of much more detailed data, this adjustment is the most appropriate available.

National totals and trends

Table 8 shows the totals for Britain of the core poor, breadline poor, asset wealthy and exclusive wealthy percentages from 1970 to 2000.[7] Poverty and wealth are, respectively, charted in Figures 1 and 2. The trends indicate that during the 1970s, levels of poverty and core poverty dropped at fairly similar rates, both declining by around a third over the decade. During the 1980s, both poverty and core poverty increased substantially, effectively reversing the improvements seen in the previous decade. From 1990-2000, the poverty level continued to rise to reach 27% of households, a level unprecedented in this study period. However, over this time period, the core poverty percentage actually dropped to return to a similar figure to that for 1980.

Table 8: Poor and wealthy households in Britain (1970-2000)

Year	% core poor	% breadline poor	% non-poor, non-wealthy	% asset wealthy	% exclusive wealthy[a]
1970	14.4	23.1			7.4
1980	9.8	17.1	66.1	16.8	6.9
1990	14.3	21.3	55.7	23.0	3.5
2000	11.2	27.0	50.4	22.6	5.6

Note: [a] See Appendix 1 for variability around the exclusive wealthy estimate. The trend is the same for each variant of the measure.

This divergence of the poverty and core poverty measures in the 1990s is fascinating. One possible explanation is that the welfare measures that were introduced to improve living conditions for the very worst off have been working, and while unemployment has been declining at the same time, more people have found themselves in low-paid work, resulting in an increase in poor households. It should be noted that the core poor are a subset of the poor, so these trends do not result simply from a large-scale shift of people from one state to the other.

Based on our analysis of housing wealth, around 17% of households were asset wealthy at the start of the 1980s. At the same time, the Family Expenditure Survey analysis indicates that around 7% of households were exclusive wealthy, a slight decrease from the figure for 1970. This estimate of 7% is around the upper limit of a range of estimates we have made for the proportion of households that are exclusive wealthy in this first analysis of the concept in Britain (see Appendix 1). Exclusive wealth is an extremely slippery concept. For instance, when we began this work in 2005 a subsidiary of Barclays Bank defined high

---

[7] Some poverty figures reported here that are based on the 1983, 1990 and 1999 Surveys have been previously reported by the JRF project 'Poverty and Social Exclusion in Britain' (Gordon et al, 2000). However, it should be noted that these figures have been slightly revised since that analysis based on updated census data and weighting methodology.

Figure 1: Change in % of households in breadline poor and core poor poverty from 1970-2000

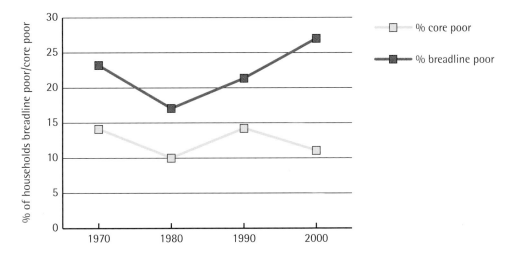

Figure 2: Change in % of asset wealthy and exclusive wealthy households from 1970/80-2000

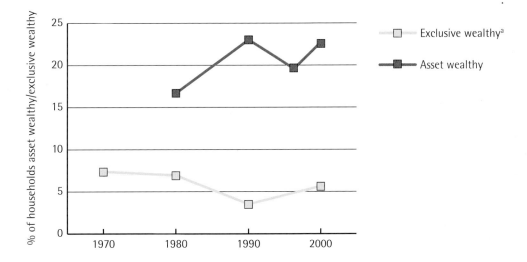

Note: [a] See Appendix 1 for variability around the exclusive wealth estimate. The trend is the same for each variant of the measure. Figures for 1970 asset wealth not available.

net worth individuals as having incomes of over £60,000 a year. A year later the figure was adjusted to £100,000.

The asset wealthy measure increased during the 1980s, but then fell during the first half of the 1990s, tying in with the economic recession (including the early 1990s' housing price crash) occurring around this time. During the latter half of the 1990s, numbers of asset wealthy households began to increase again, to return to almost 1990 levels by 2000. The proportion of households classified as exclusive wealthy declined slightly during the 1970s and more sharply during the 1980s. In other words, the very wealthy became a smaller and more exclusive group over this period. During the 1990s, the exclusive wealthy measure began to increase to reach around 5% by 2000.

Finally, Table 8 indicates a steady decrease in the proportion of households classified as neither poor nor wealthy from 1980-2000. This simple finding would indicate an increasingly polarised Britain, an issue that is explored in depth through the remainder of this report.

National maps and geographical changes over time

Poverty

Maps 1 and 2 show the geographical patterns of the poverty and core poverty measures, and how these change between 1970 and 2000. Each set of maps has been coloured using a common scale, in order to be able to see the changes across the decades. For each year, there is a pair of maps, which are coloured in exactly the same way. The traditional map on the left of the pair uses geographical boundaries. However, these make it very hard to see what is happening within cities, as urban areas are geographically very small. The cartogram on the right of the pair addresses this by making each tract equal in area (depicted by half a hexagon). This distorts the image from the traditional view, but gives a much clearer picture, especially of urban poverty. Since each tract contains roughly the same population, the cartogram is a much 'fairer' view of population statistics, effectively according each person the same space on the map.

Map 1 shows the proportion of households classified as breadline poor mainly varying between about 10% and 30%, with higher rates tending to be in the north of England, Wales and Scotland. Higher rates of 30-40% are only found in Central London, cities of the North and the West Midlands of England, and Scotland, especially Glasgow, and the valleys of South Wales. By 1980, poverty levels decreased almost everywhere, with high pockets remaining in London, Glasgow, and some cities of northern England. Areas with poverty levels below 10% were much more prevalent in 1980 than in 1970. This trend is reversed by 1990, with the map resembling that of 1970, with even higher levels, especially in Glasgow and the West Midlands. The trend of the 1980s continues through the 1990s, with the map for 2000 showing levels above 50% occurring in a number of cities, and no areas remain with breadline poverty levels below 10%.

Spatial patterns of core poverty, demonstrated in Map 2, reflect those of poverty from 1970 to 1990. However, by 2000, core poverty levels declined across most of Britain, with high levels remaining in the areas with high poverty levels: Central London, Glasgow, and cities of the West Midlands and north of England. It is interesting to note that while the overall levels of core poverty in 1970 and 1990 are very similar, at around 14%, the geographical patterns are very different. In 1970, there were fewer areas with levels below 10%, and small pockets of levels above 20% only found within some inner-city areas. In 1990, the urban clustering is much more pronounced, with more tracts at less than 10%, and inner-city pockets above 20% larger and more widespread. Similar overall levels of core poverty in 1980 and 2000 are again distributed differently, with more urban clusters of high levels in 2000. These spatial patterns are explored further in the section on spatial clustering below.

Map 1: The changing geography of breadline poverty (1970-2000)

1970

1980

1990

2000

Breadline poor %

< 10.1
10.1 - 20.0
20.1 - 30.0
30.1 - 40.0
40.1 - 50.0
50.1 - 70.0

Maps illustrate the percentage of households classified as breadline poor at the relevant time period

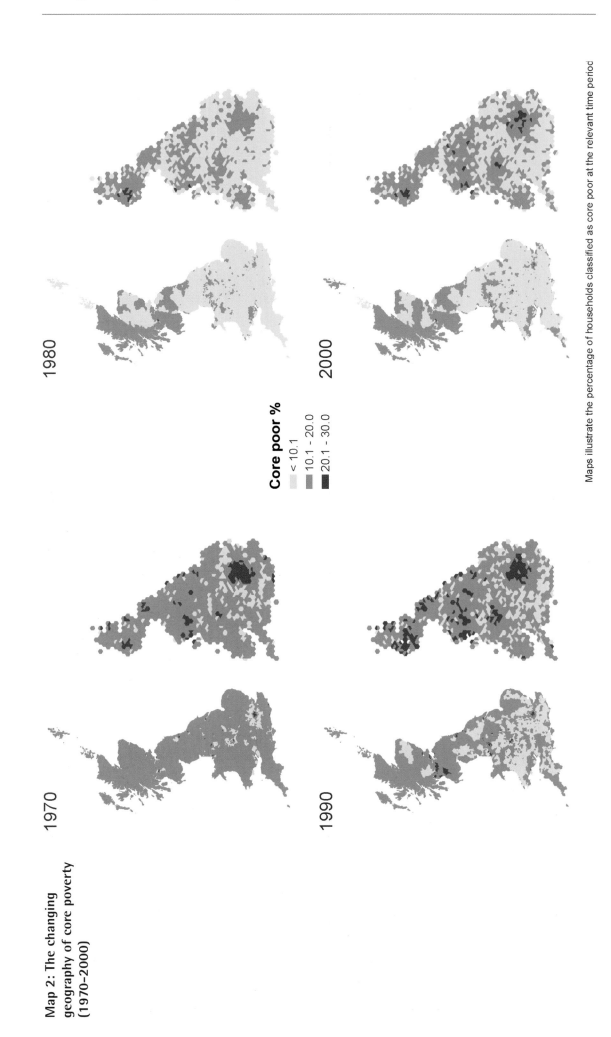

Map 2: The changing geography of core poverty (1970–2000)

1970

1980

1990

2000

Core poor %

< 10.1

10.1 - 20.0

20.1 - 30.0

Maps illustrate the percentage of households classified as core poor at the relevant time period

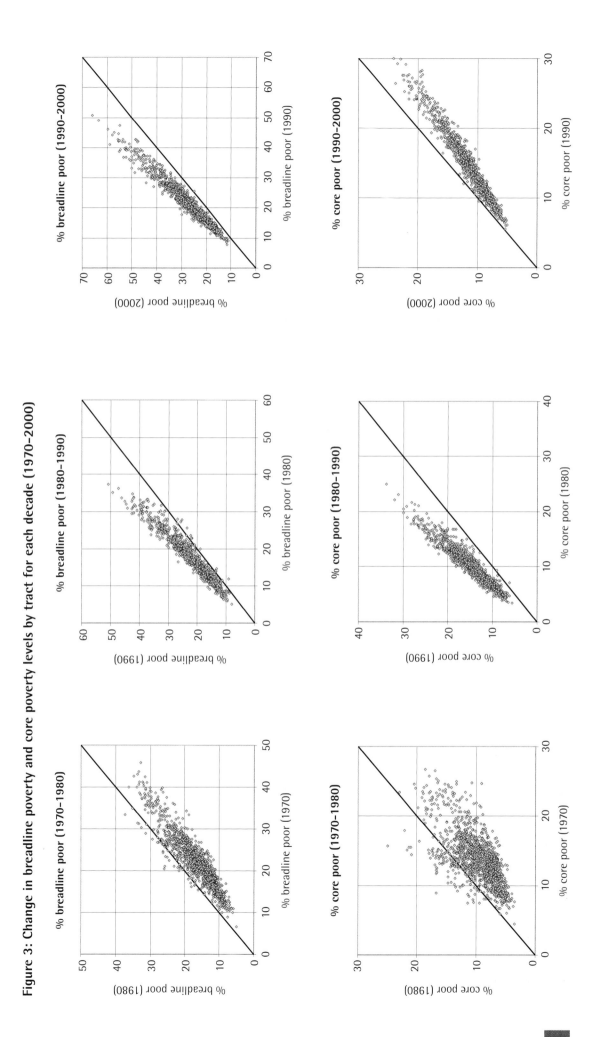

Figure 3: Change in breadline poverty and core poverty levels by tract for each decade (1970–2000)

The graphs of Figure 3 demonstrate the change in breadline and core poverty levels for each tract across each decade. The percentage of breadline poor households decreased in almost every tract between 1970 and 1980; on average for every seven poor households in a tract in 1970, there were six by 1980. The three tracts with the largest decreases[8] over the decade were all in Scottish cities: Aberdeen Queens Cross (perhaps reflecting new found wealth from the oil industry), Edinburgh North and Edinburgh Holyrood. Only 32 of the 1,282 tracts showed an increase in household poverty over the 1970s, and the top three were Livingston Central (near Edinburgh), Weaver Vale North (Cheshire) and Glasgow Easterhouse.

The equivalent graph for the 1980s is almost a mirror image of that for the 1970s. Only 15 tracts had a decline in the poverty rate over the decade, the largest declines being in Balerno (outskirts of Edinburgh), Battersea East and Tooting West (both in London, likely to have been experiencing gentrification at this time). All other tracts experienced an increase in poverty rates, with an average of six poor households in 1990 for every five in 1980. The greatest increases were in Tyne Bridge West (Newcastle upon Tyne), Glasgow Easterhouse and Glasgow Milton. The Tyne Bridge West tract is that part of the constituency north of the Tyne that would have been experiencing deindustrialisation, including areas such as Scotswood and Benwell.

The pattern of change across tracts during the 1990s was very similar to that of the 1980s. During this decade, only one tract saw a fall in poverty – Sidlaw and Carnoustie (Dundee), which experienced a small decline, from 25.7 to 24.9%. The three largest increases were in Hodge Hill West (inner-city Birmingham), and two London tracts, East Ham North and Camberwell Green.

Maps of change in each decade are presented in Appendix 2.

Wealth

Maps 3 and 4 show the changing geographical patterns of asset wealth and exclusive wealth, through the 1980s and 1990s. At the start of the 1980s, asset wealthy households are concentrated in southern England, and more generally elsewhere in rural parts of the country, notably north Devon, rural exclaves of the West Midlands and mid-Wales. This rural bias is perhaps inevitable given the higher prevalence of home ownership outside of urban areas, but this does reflect actual owned wealth above a national threshold, and so is an accurate portrayal. The pattern in 1990 is very similar, although with higher levels of wealth reflecting the higher national total (23% compared to 17% in 1980). By the mid-1990s, the pattern starts to take on a more South East-centric concentration. Overall wealth levels have fallen to under 20%, and the highest levels of wealth are concentrated in a smaller area around the south and west of London, along with a few other small pockets nationally. By 2000, it is apparent that while total asset wealth levels have again risen, wealth continues to be concentrated in the south east of England. Comparing the two cartograms for 1990 and 2000 make this especially obvious (the national total at both times is very similar). The maps of the change over each time period (presented in Appendix 2) demonstrate this further, particularly for the period 1990-96, when the overall asset wealth rate was falling, but the proportions of asset wealthy households were increasing across much of the south east.

---

[8] Decreases and increases mentioned here are absolute – that is, an increase from 30-40% (absolute increase of 10%, relative increase of 33%) is counted as greater than an increase from 5-14% (absolute increase of 9%, relative increase of 180%).

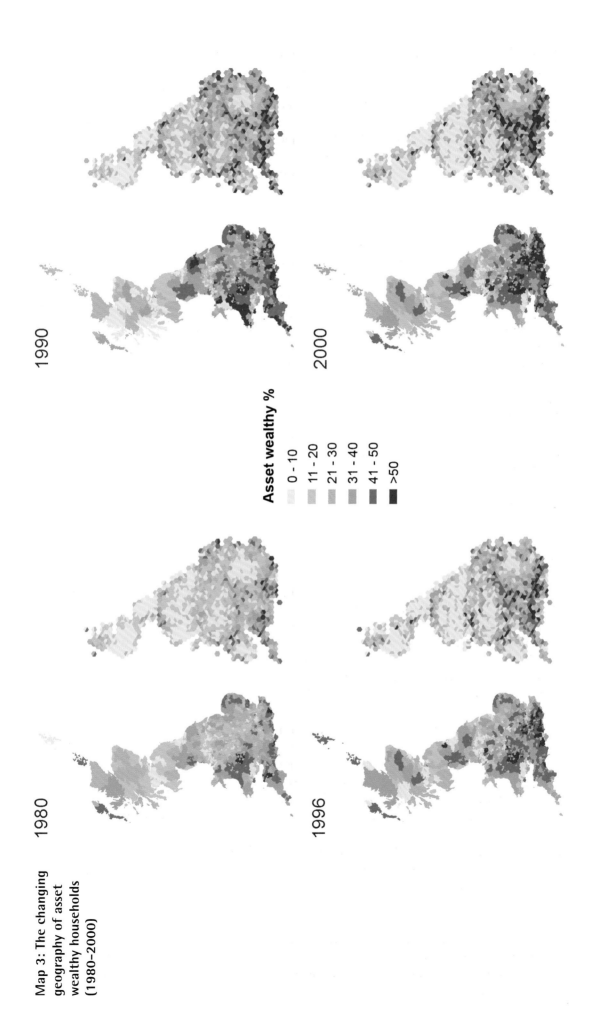

Map 3: The changing geography of asset wealthy households (1980–2000)

1980

1990

1996

2000

Asset wealthy %

0 - 10
11 - 20
21 - 30
31 - 40
41 - 50
>50

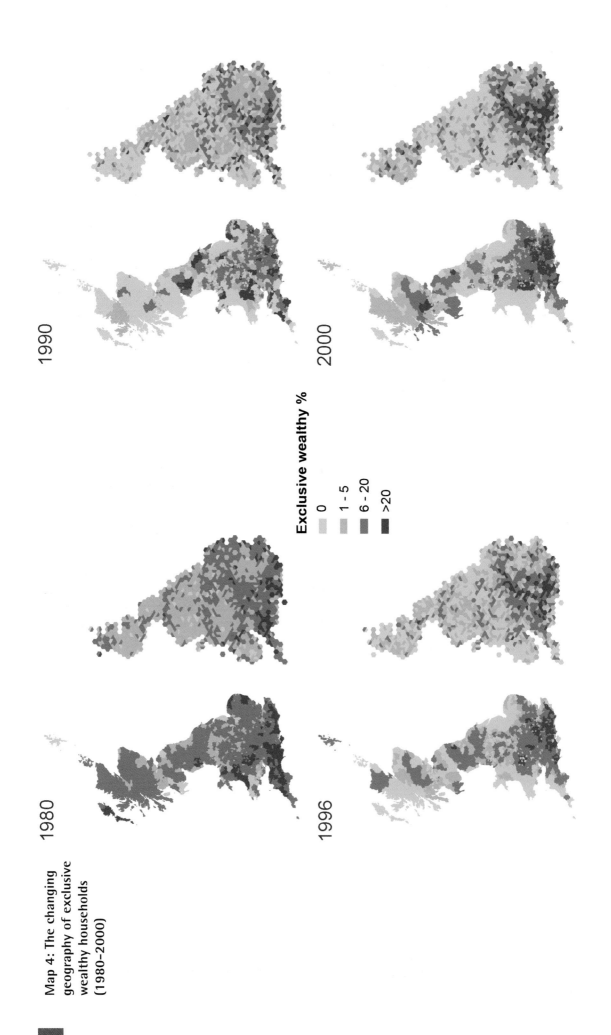

Map 4: The changing geography of exclusive wealthy households (1980–2000)

Exclusive wealthy %

0
1 - 5
6 - 20
>20

1980

1990

1996

2000

Maps of exclusive wealthy households show similar geographical patterns developing over time, becoming increasingly concentrated in the immediate vicinity of London, and increasingly absent from much of the rest of Britain.[9] This concentration is especially the case during the 1990s. It should be noted that the national proportion of exclusive wealthy households used to calibrate local estimates for 1996 was estimated as the mean of 1990 and 2000 values.

The scatter plots of Figure 4 show the change in asset wealth and exclusive wealth rates for each tract during the 1980s, the first half of the 1990s, and the latter half of the 1990s. These do not present such obvious patterns as those for poverty in Figure 3 above. The general trend is for tracts with many asset wealthy households in 1980 to still have many in 1990, with most tracts experiencing a modest increase over the decade. During the early 1990s, many tracts experience a decline in asset wealthy rate (the map of change in Appendix 2 gives greater insight into where the rate rose and fell). The trend is then somewhat reversed during the late 1990s. The patterns are clearest in the last period, when we are using near-100% data from the Land Registry (see Thomas and Dorling, 2004). The patterns for exclusive wealthy households are less clear, although they reflect the national changes to some extent, with declining rates during the 1980s in most tracts. It should be noted that these patterns may also be affected by the fixed nature of the assets, including housing wealth, which is non-portable.

Non-poor, non-wealthy

The number of households classified neither as (asset) wealthy nor (breadline) poor declines over the decades, from 66% in 1980, to 56% in 1990, and 50% in 2000 (see Table 8). This 'middle' section of the population is of interest, since areas with few wealthy and few poor people could be thought of as the least unequal or polarised. Map 5 illustrates the geographical distribution of this 'middle' group of households.

The geographical distribution reflects the overall decline in the prevalence of non-poor, non-wealthy households, although it appears to become an increasingly clear north/south pattern. By 2000, the lowest proportions of non-poor, non-wealthy households are almost all found in London and southern England, and the highest proportions are in southern Wales and northern England.

---

[9] Since there are a large number of tracts with no exclusive wealthy households, these are given their own category on the map.

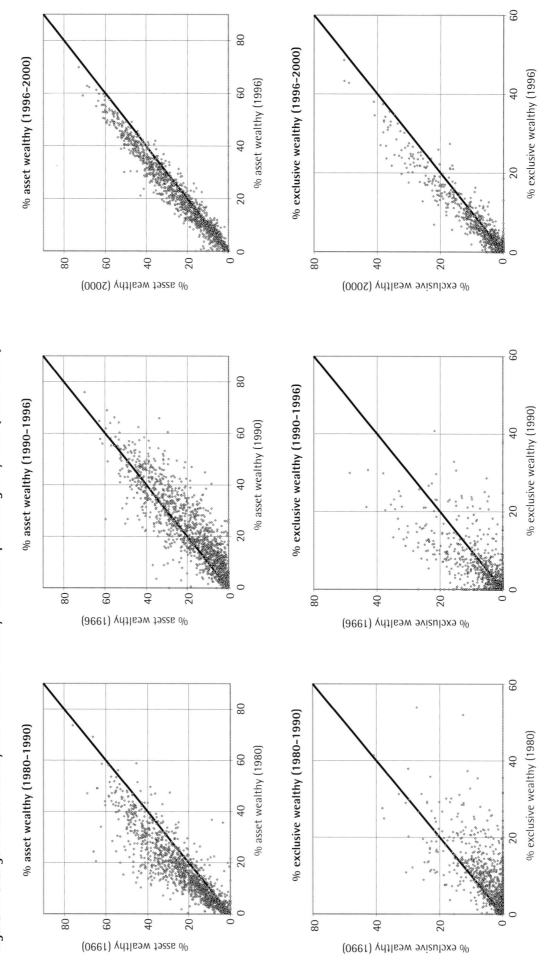

Figure 4: Change in asset wealthy and exclusive wealthy household percentages by tract (1980–2000)

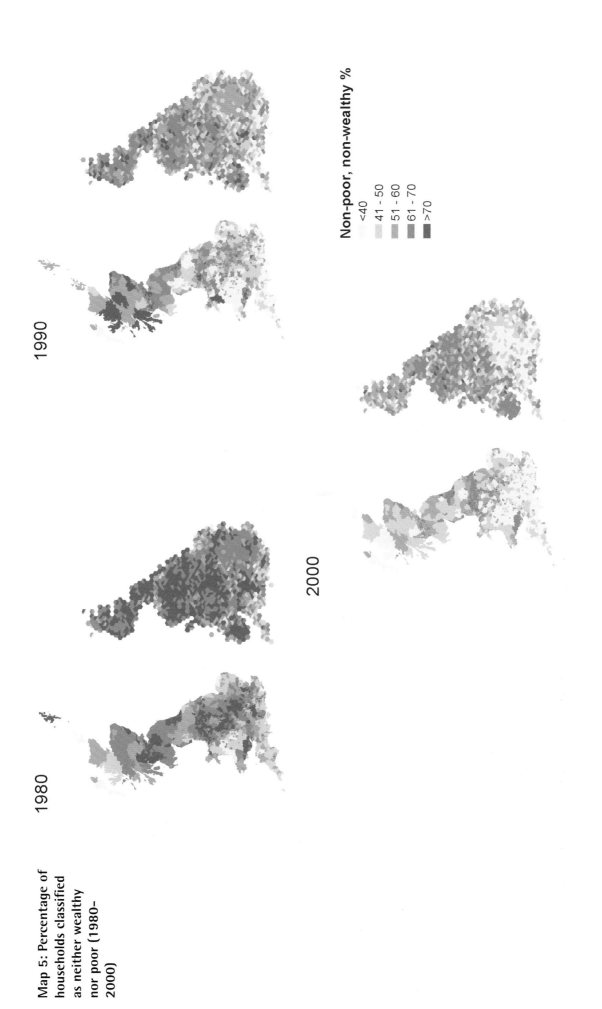

Map 5: Percentage of households classified as neither wealthy nor poor (1980–2000)

1980

1990

2000

Non-poor, non-wealthy %

<40
41 - 50
51 - 60
61 - 70
>70

Polarisation and spatial concentration

Polarisation

At its most basic, social and spatial polarisation can be broadly defined as the widening gap between groups of people in terms of their economic and social circumstances and opportunities. (Dorling and Woodward, 1996, p 71)

An assessment of the degree of polarisation and how this changes over time is a fundamental element of this study. For the first time, we have available a coherent time series of consistently calculated poverty and wealth measures for the same set of small areas across Britain. As illustrated above, it is interesting to look at the overall rates and geographical patterns of poverty and wealth over the past 30 or 40 years. However, the changing degree of polarisation is perhaps of greater significance with respect to the impacts of changing public policy on social inequalities in Britain.

Poverty

In order to assess the changing degree of polarisation, we replicate the method introduced by Dorling and Woodward (1996) a decade ago. The method constructs a histogram of the distribution of the population across tract breadline poverty rates (in this case) across all tracts for each time period. To construct the histograms, a series of categories or 'bins' of poverty rates are defined, and the population in tracts falling into each bin calculated. The histograms for two time periods can then be subtracted from each other to calculate the changing distribution of the population by tract poverty rate.

This method is perhaps best understood with reference to Table 9 and Figures 5 and 6. For this analysis, 14 categories of breadline poverty rates were constructed around a central rate of 20%. Twenty per cent was selected based on the overall poverty rates described above, but the absolute value of this figure makes little difference to the resulting graphs. The 14 categories were mirrored around the central 20% rate, for example category 1 includes those tracts where less than 10% (0.5 × 20%) of households are poor. Category 14 includes the tracts where more than 40% (2 × 20%) of households are poor. The same 14 categories were used for each time period to produce the population distribution histogram across tracts by poverty rate. These histograms were then compared to investigate the changing distribution of the population across tract poverty rates.

Table 9 contains the data used to produce the graphs in Figures 5 and 6. The column for 1970 shows that 0.19% of the population lived in category 1 tracts; those where less than 10% of households were breadline poor. By 1980, 7.5% of the population lived in category 1 tracts, an absolute increase of 7.3% in the population in this category. The equivalent change for the population living in category 14 tracts, where 40% or more

Table 9: Distribution of contemporary population across tracts categorised by breadline poverty density (% poor households in each tract), for each time period, the change over each decade, and the change 1970–2000

Category	Bin, relative to 20%	Percentage of households classified as breadline poor	% of population in each category				Change in % of population in each category			
			1970	1980	1990	2000	1970 to 1980	1980 to 1990	1990 to 2000	1970 to 2000
1	Less than 0.5×	Less than 10	0.19	7.50	0.88	0.00	7.31	-6.62	-0.88	-0.19
2	0.5 to 0.67×	10 to 13.3	4.72	22.77	9.63	1.01	18.05	-13.15	-8.62	-3.72
3	0.67 to 0.71×	13.3 to 14.3	1.98	8.58	6.68	1.37	6.60	-1.89	-5.31	-0.61
4	0.71 to 0.77×	14.3 to 15.4	3.35	7.75	5.48	1.88	4.41	-2.27	-3.60	-1.46
5	0.77 to 0.83×	15.4 to 16.7	5.62	7.78	9.14	5.31	2.16	1.37	-3.84	-0.32
6	0.83 to 0.91×	16.7 to 18.2	8.70	8.71	9.06	7.34	0.00	0.36	-1.72	-1.36
7	0.91 to 1×	18.2 to 20	10.48	8.95	10.12	8.21	-1.53	1.16	-1.91	-2.28
8	1 to 1.1×	20 to 22	14.74	8.84	10.32	10.67	-5.91	1.48	0.35	-4.07
9	1.1 to 1.2×	22 to 24	11.56	5.54	8.81	8.87	-6.02	3.27	0.06	-2.69
10	1.2 to 1.3×	24 to 26	9.72	4.70	6.82	8.65	-5.01	2.11	1.84	-1.07
11	1.3 to 1.4×	26 to 28	9.71	3.34	7.13	8.08	-6.37	3.79	0.95	-1.63
12	1.4 to 1.5×	28 to 30	6.03	2.04	3.28	7.88	-3.99	1.23	4.60	1.84
13	1.5 to 2×	30 to 40	12.09	3.49	11.20	21.14	-8.60	7.71	9.94	9.05
14	2× and above	40 to 100	1.10	0.00	1.45	9.60	-1.10	1.45	8.15	8.50
Total		0 to 100	100	100	100	100	0	0	0	0

Figure 5: Spatial polarisation of the population by tract breadline poverty density during the 1970s, 1980s and 1990s

x-axis categories, constructed around a central poverty rate of 20%

1: Proportion of population living in tracts with less than half (<0.5x) the central poverty rate (ie tracts where <10% households are poor)
2: 0.5–0.67x

3: 0.67–0.71x
4: 0.71–0.77x
5: 0.77–0.83x
6: 0.83–0.91x
7: 0.91–1x

8: 1–1.1x
9: 1.1–1.2x
10: 1.2–1.3x
11: 1.3–1.4x
12: 1.4–1.5x

13: 1.5–2x
14: Proportion of population living in tracts with more than twice (>2x) the central poverty rate (ie tracts where >40% of households are poor)1: Proportion of households are poor)

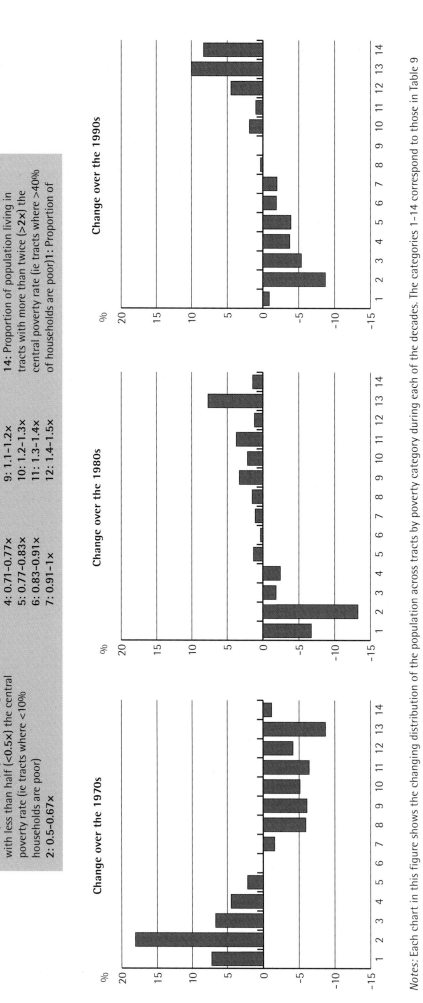

Change over the 1970s

Change over the 1980s

Change over the 1990s

Notes: Each chart in this figure shows the changing distribution of the population across tracts by poverty category during each of the decades. The categories 1–14 correspond to those in Table 9 and listed above. For example, the bar for category 1 in the leftmost chart shows that from 1970–1980, the proportion of the population in Britain that lived in tracts where less than 10% of households were poor increased by about 7%. The bar for category 14 in the same chart shows that during the same time period, the proportion of the population living in tracts where more than 40% of households were poor declined by around 1%. The overall change from 1970–2000 is shown in Figure 6.
Each graph uses the same vertical scale in order that comparisons can be made across decades.

of households were breadline poor, was from 1.1% in 1970 to 0% in 1980, an absolute decrease of 1.1%. These changes in the proportion of the population in the breadline poverty rate categories are the figures graphed in Figures 5 and 6.

The figures in Table 9 are hard to interpret, but once in graphical form, overall patterns are clearly visible. The first graph in Figure 5 shows that from 1970-80, the proportion of the population living in areas with relatively low levels of breadline poverty increased substantially, while the population living in areas with relatively high levels of poverty decreased substantially. This indicates that in terms of household poverty, Britain's population became substantially less concentrated in areas of high poverty during the 1970s. Areas became more similar in terms of poverty rates. However, the graph for the 1980s shows the opposite to be the case – especially in areas with very high levels of poverty – and this trend continued through the 1990s. More and more people became concentrated in enclaves of high poverty.

It is worth noting here that the trend of the 1990s is the opposite of that discovered in recent research on the US. Jargowsky (2003) found that despite the numbers of poor people in the US rising from 31.7 million to 33.9 million between 1990 and 2000, the number of high-poverty neighbourhoods where over 40% of the population were poor declined by a quarter. Poverty appeared to have become more prevalent, but much less concentrated in the US, whereas these findings for the same time period indicate increasing poverty prevalence and concentration in the UK.

Figure 6 shows the overall change in the population distribution across tract poverty categories from 1970-2000. The population living in the highest three categories of tract – those where 28% or more of households were poor – increased, especially in the top two categories. The proportion of the population living in all tracts with lower poverty rates decreased over the 30-year period.

Figure 6: Spatial polarisation of the population by tract breadline poverty density across the study period (1970–2000)

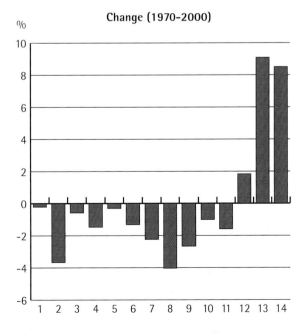

Notes: Category 1: tracts where less than 10% of households are breadline poor; category 14: tracts where more than 40% of households are breadline poor.

Figure 6 shows that, in total, over the course of the 30 years 1970-2000, the only types of area to increase in population in Britain were those in which 28% or more of households were poor (categories 12, 13 and 14).

The UK trend may have various causal mechanisms operating behind it. One possibility could be that poorer populations have been growing fastest in poor areas, replacing households that were more average, but which had dissolved, left or died, or that more affluent people have been moving out of poor areas to more wealthy places (we discuss the issue of migration in Chapter 9). The mechanisms, and possibly the trends, are likely to vary from place to place.

Given that this is not a longitudinal study, we are unable to track the movement of poor (or wealthy) people over the time series. However, to gain some understanding of population changes over time with respect to poor areas, we have measured the change in population of tracts according to their levels of poverty at the earliest time available (a similar analysis using the asset wealth measure is presented below). Figure 7 shows the population change for tracts by decile of the 1970 Breadline Poverty Index over each following decade. Each decile contained roughly the same population in 1971; by 2001, the tracts in the poorest 1970 decile had lost over 20% of their population. Over the same time period, the tracts in the least poor decile had experienced an increase in population of nearly 20%. Looking at these changes decade by decade shows that while the population gain of the least poor areas is fairly steady, most of the population loss in the poorest tracts occurred in the 1970s. A much smaller degree of loss occurred in the 1980s in the poorest three deciles, and this reversed over the 1990s to produce small population increases in those tracts by 2001. In some areas this might be attributable to processes of gentrification.

Figure 7: Change in population of tracts by 1970 breadline poverty decile from 1971-2001

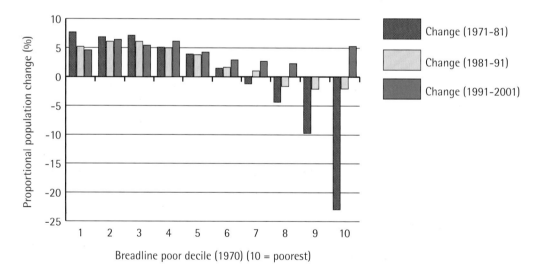

The finding of a small increase in population in the poorest areas during the 1990s is supported when we analyse the change over this decade according to the 1990 Breadline Poverty Index (as opposed to that for 1970), although the observed increase is smaller. The poorest decile of tracts by the 1990 Index experienced an increase in population of 0.9% between 1991 and 2001. This increase may well be explained by the tendency for the populations of poorer areas to have much younger age structures, and consequently for losses due to deaths and migration to be outweighed by birth and immigration gains.

Wealth

> The stratosphere of the boardrooms, where the likes of Lord Browne of BP now
> earn £6.5m a year, has moved as far from the life of the average citizen as the
> addict in a blanket under Waterloo Bridge. They no longer inhabit the same planet
> as the rest of us, hermetically sealed in smoke-windowed limo, private jet, private
> island, private everything. (Toynbee, 2006)

The polarisation analysis of breadline poverty rates described above was repeated
using the time series of the percentage of asset wealthy households in each tract. The
14 categories were constructed as mirrored bins around a central figure of 20% asset
wealthy, again chosen with reference to the overall totals in Table 8. As with the poverty
polarisation analysis, the value selected here makes little difference to the results, so long
as it is roughly similar to the overall total asset wealth percentage figures. Table 10 shows
the figures used to construct the graphs in Figures 8 and 9.

The graphs indicate that during the 1980s, Britain's population became increasingly
polarised with respect to the distribution of asset wealthy households. By 1990, more
people lived in areas with more wealthy households, and fewer people lived in areas
with fewer wealthy households. This trend dramatically reversed during the first half of
the 1990s, undoubtedly associated with the tremendous loss of wealth affecting some of
those with most to lose in the recession and housing market crash at that time. The effect
of this 'economic downturn' was actually to make Britain appear much more equal with
respect to asset wealth. It is unclear what the 'felt' impact of this dramatic change would
have been. If the housing market is viewed as cyclical, but with an overall upward trend,
and if almost all of the wealthy maintained ownership of their houses despite falling values
during this time, then perceived changes in polarisation may be much smaller than actual
changes. Previous research has shown that negative equity did hit the poor hardest at this
time (Dorling et al, 1994).

The last graph in the sequence, for the late 1990s, shows another reversal of the trend to
one similar to the 1980s. Figure 9 indicates that the trend of the early 1990s is outweighed
by the changes at other times over the two decades. There was an overall increase in
the population living in the areas with the highest density of wealthy households, and a
decrease in the population living in areas with fewer wealthy households over the 20-year
period (this chart is brought up to date in the section on 'Wealth', Chapter 8, page 76).

The analysis of population change for tracts by breadline poverty decile illustrated in
Figure 7 was repeated for tracts by 1980 asset wealthy decile. The graph in Figure 10
shows a similar pattern to that produced using the poverty measure. Relatively large
declines in population occurred in the least wealthy deciles during the 1980s, but this
decline almost stopped or reversed slightly in the 1990s. The wealthier tracts in 1980
gained population over the following 20 years. Overall, the population of those tracts in
the wealthiest decile increased by around 15%, while tracts in the least wealthy decile lost
around 2% of their population.

Table 10: Distribution of contemporary population across tracts categorised by asset wealth density (% asset wealthy households in each tract), for each time period, the change over each decade, and the change 1980–2000

Category	Bin, relative to 20%	Percentage of households classified as breadline poor	% of population in each category				Change in % of population in each category			
			1980	1990	1996ᵃ	2000	1980 to 1990	1990 to 1996	1996 to 2000	1980 to 2000
1	Less than 0.5x	Less than 10	35.3	22.1	34.4	31.3	-13.3	12.3	-3.0	-4.0
2	0.5 to 0.67x	10 to 13.3	12.6	9.2	8.6	6.2	-3.4	-0.7	-2.4	-6.4
3	0.67 to 0.71x	13.3 to 14.3	3.0	2.4	1.9	1.8	-0.7	-0.5	0.0	-1.2
4	0.71 to 0.77x	14.3 to 15.4	3.6	2.7	2.2	2.2	-0.9	-0.5	0.0	-1.4
5	0.77 to 0.83x	15.4 to 16.7	2.7	3.5	2.7	3.1	0.8	-0.8	0.4	0.4
6	0.83 to 0.91x	16.7 to 18.2	3.9	4.4	3.4	2.6	0.5	-1.0	-0.8	-1.4
7	0.91 to 1x	18.2 to 20	5.7	4.9	3.4	3.2	-0.8	-1.5	-0.1	-2.4
8	1 to 1.1x	20 to 22	5.2	3.3	4.3	3.7	-1.9	1.0	-0.6	-1.5
9	1.1 to 1.2x	22 to 24	4.2	4.9	3.4	3.6	0.8	-1.5	0.2	-0.6
10	1.2 to 1.3x	24 to 26	3.8	4.1	3.1	2.7	0.3	-1.0	-0.4	-1.1
11	1.3 to 1.4x	26 to 28	2.3	3.7	3.5	3.4	1.4	-0.3	-0.1	1.0
12	1.4 to 1.5x	28 to 30	2.7	3.3	4.0	3.0	0.6	0.6	-1.0	0.3
13	1.5 to 2x	30 to 40	10.0	16.2	13.3	15.7	6.2	-2.9	2.4	5.7
14	2x and above	40 to 100	5.0	15.3	12.0	17.5	10.3	-3.3	5.5	12.5
Total		0 to 100	100	100	100	100	0	0	0	0

Note: ᵃ The population for each tract for 1996 was estimated as the mean of the 1991 and 2001 Census populations.

Figure 8: Spatial polarisation of the population by tract asset wealthy density during the 1980s and 1990s

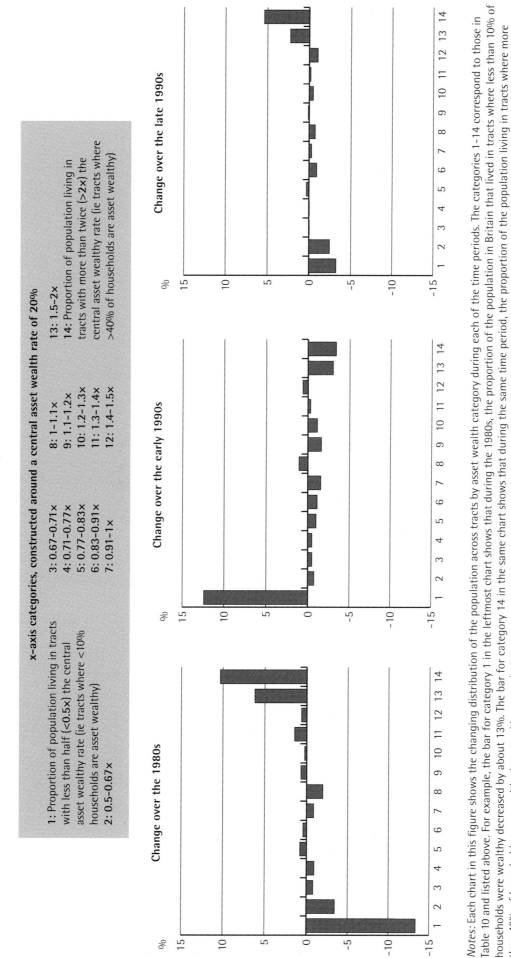

x-axis categories, constructed around a central asset wealth rate of 20%

1: Proportion of population living in tracts with less than half (<0.5x) the central asset wealth rate (ie tracts where <10% households are asset wealthy)

2: 0.5–0.67x

3: 0.67–0.71x
4: 0.71–0.77x
5: 0.77–0.83x
6: 0.83–0.91x
7: 0.91–1x

8: 1–1.1x
9: 1.1–1.2x
10: 1.2–1.3x
11: 1.3–1.4x
12: 1.4–1.5x

13: 1.5–2x
14: Proportion of population living in tracts with more than twice (>2x) the central asset wealthy rate (ie tracts where >40% of households are asset wealthy)

Notes: Each chart in this figure shows the changing distribution of the population across tracts by asset wealth category during each of the time periods. The categories 1–14 correspond to those in Table 10 and listed above. For example, the bar for category 1 in the leftmost chart shows that during the 1980s, the proportion of the population in Britain that lived in tracts where less than 10% of households were wealthy decreased by about 13%. The bar for category 14 in the same chart shows that during the same time period, the proportion of the population living in tracts where more than 40% of households were wealthy increased by around 10%. The overall change from 1980–2000 is shown in Figure 9. Each graph uses the same vertical scale in order that comparisons can be made across decades.

Figure 9: Spatial polarisation of the population by tract asset wealthy density (1980-2000)

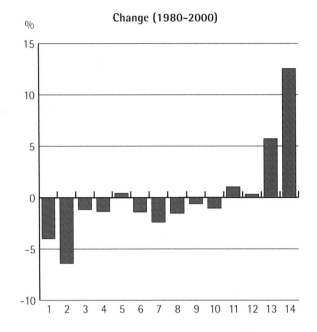

Notes: Category 1: tracts where less than 10% of households are asset wealthy; category 14: tracts where more than 40% of households are asset wealthy. See Figure 8, page 35, for full details of the 14 categories.

Figure 10: Change in population of tracts by 1980 asset wealthy decile from 1981–2001

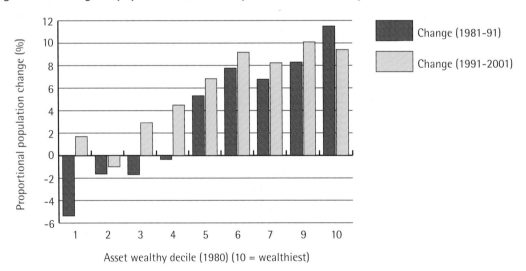

Spatial clustering

> Everything is related to everything else, but near things are more related than distant things. (Waldo Tobler's 'First law of geography'; Tobler, 1970, p 236)

The geographical patterns of poverty and wealth across time can be observed simply by looking at the maps elsewhere in this report. However, spatial statistics can be used to further investigate and describe the spatial distribution, particularly the degree of spatial concentration, of poor and wealthy households. For example, statistics can be calculated that indicate the extent to which areas with high levels of poverty tend to be found near to other areas with high levels of poverty. The statistics and maps presented in this section effectively measure how similar or dissimilar each area is to its neighbours, giving an indication of the degree of spatial concentration of poverty and wealth.

An extensive literature exists on the methodology and application of this kind of spatial analysis; it is not appropriate to dwell on this here. A standard measure of spatial association (spatial autocorrelation) is Moran's I statistic. Whereas with a standard correlation measure we seek to investigate the extent of association between two variables, or characteristics, with spatial autocorrelation we explore how similar the characteristic of one area is compared with its close neighbours, and with more distant areas. The geographical measure gives an indication of the extent to which, across the whole study area, neighbouring areas are similar with respect to this characteristic. A further refinement to this approach is to calculate the spatial association measure on a more localised basis, resulting in a map of 'spatial clusters' of similar areas. A recent study used these 'Local Indicators of Spatial Association' (LISA) (Anselin, 1995) techniques to investigate the spatial concentration of poverty in 1896 and 1991 using a social class measure (Orford, 2004). In this section, we describe similar exploratory analyses of the time series data, using LISA to investigate the changing spatial concentration of poverty and wealth across Britain. Details of the software and methodology used are given in Appendix 1.

Poverty

The global spatial autocorrelation statistic (Moran's I and associated p-values) for breadline poor and core poor percentages across all tracts are detailed in Table 11. The statistic can be interpreted in a very similar manner to a correlation coefficient. Higher positive values indicate that neighbouring areas are more similar to each other than to those further away; larger negative values indicate that neighbouring areas tend to be dissimilar; 0 indicates little or no spatial association. A simulation-based p-value can be calculated, which indicates the likelihood that the actual value of Moran's I is 0.

Table 11: Global Moran's I statistics for breadline poor and core poor measures[a]

	Breadline poor	Core poor
1970	0.5952	0.5548
1980	0.5844	0.5507
1990	0.5686	0.5602
2000	0.5590	0.5592

Note: [a] All p-values < 0.001.

All of the Moran's I statistics are around 0.5-0.6, indicating quite a strong degree of positive spatial association; neighbouring areas tend to have similar breadline poverty and core poverty rates. There is little change over the decades, although there is an apparent trend for the breadline poor Moran's I to decrease slightly over time. This trend is fairly weak, but suggests that the degree of spatial clustering of breadline poverty rates overall may be declining over time. Note that Moran's I is a global indicator. What appears to be happening, when we consider local measures (see below), is that the effect of higher rates of poverty coalescing in the poorer urban areas is outweighed by increasing mild heterogeneity elsewhere, which is not so visually obvious.

Maps 6 and 7 show the degree of spatial concentration of the breadline poor and core poor measures across the decades using LISA – effectively a local Moran's I is calculated

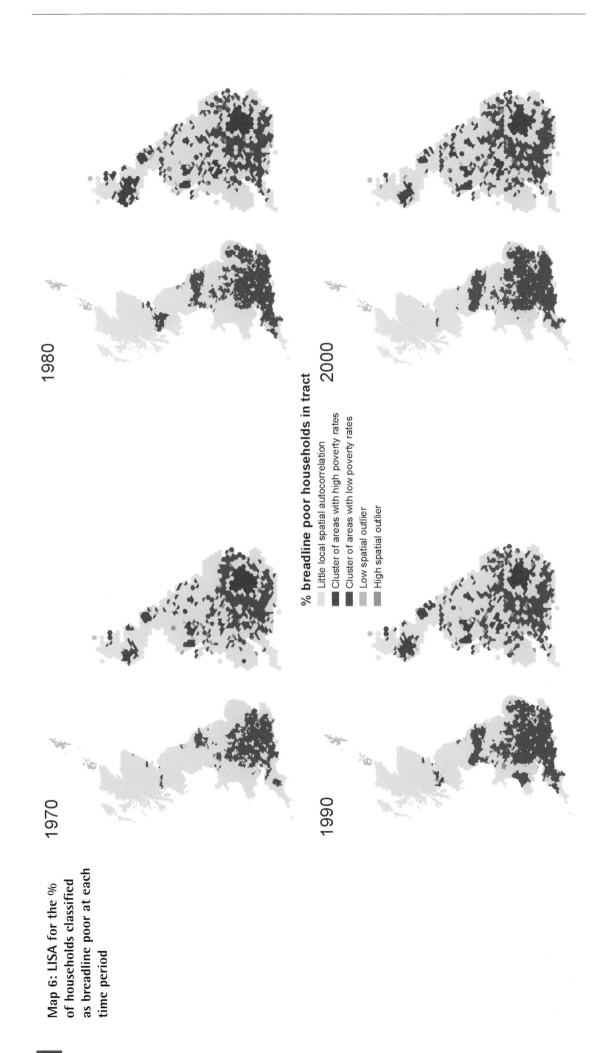

Map 6: LISA for the % of households classified as breadline poor at each time period

1970

1980

1990

2000

% breadline poor households in tract

Little local spatial autocorrelation

Cluster of areas with high poverty rates

Cluster of areas with low poverty rates

Low spatial outlier

High spatial outlier

Map 7: LISA for the % of households classified as core poor at each time period

1970

1980

1990

2000

% core poor households in tract

Little local spatial autocorrelation

Cluster of areas with high core poverty rates

Cluster of areas with low core poverty rates

Low spatial outlier

High spatial outlier

for each tract based on other tracts in proximity. The LISA analysis evaluates each tract with its neighbours in turn, and classifies each tract into one of five categories:

- *High rate cluster (red):* these are tracts that have a relatively high percentage of households in poverty that neighbour other tracts with high poverty rates.
- *Low rate cluster (dark blue):* these are tracts that have a relatively low percentage of households in poverty that neighbour other tracts with low poverty rates.
- *Low spatial outlier (light blue):* these are tracts that have a low poverty rate, but neighbour tracts with relatively high rates.
- *High spatial outlier (pink):* these are tracts that have a high poverty rate, but neighbour tracts with relatively low rates.
- *No local spatial association (grey):* these are tracts that do not demonstrate any particular similarity or dissimilarity to those around them.

The results for both breadline poor and core poor households are fairly similar, and in terms of high and low clusters are perhaps what we might expect given the maps presented previously. It should be noted here that these methods are exploratory, and issues of statistical significance are discussed briefly in Appendix 1. In 1970, poverty clusters were apparent in central London, South Wales, and cities of the West Midlands, northern England, and Scotland. Low poverty rates were clustered in the south east, south central and central England, along with a cluster in north/east Yorkshire. The pattern of high and low clusters remains similar at each time period, although there is some suggestion that high poverty clusters became larger during the 1970s and 1980s, but then decreased in extent by 2000. The cluster of low poverty rates in north/east Yorkshire appears to become more extensive over time, spreading west through rural Lancashire and parts of Cumbria. It is interesting to note that adjacent to this low poverty cluster are two notable 'high spatial outliers' (places with high poverty rates adjacent to low poverty clusters) that appear in 1980, 1990 and 2000 – Preston East and York City East.

The most prominent breadline poor clusters appearing at every time period are detailed in Table 12. The boundaries of these clusters are fluid, meaning that the counts of households are based on the extent of the cluster at that time, not a fixed definition of a city/region. This means that the geographical coverage of each named cluster is not constant over time. The table shows that, for example, the total number of households in the Inner London high poverty cluster decreased during the 1970s and 1980s, but increased again during the 1990s. However, the poverty rate within the London cluster decreased during the 1970s, and then increased during the 1980s and 1990s.

The graphs in Figure 11 support the maps in suggesting that the number of tracts in high breadline poverty clusters increased during the 1970s, but then declined during the 1980s and 1990s. While this analysis is exploratory, it does support the argument that poverty became increasingly geographically concentrated during the latter two decades; poverty rates increased overall, but the geographical clusters contracted.

One specific limitation of this type of cluster analysis is that it is affected by 'edges' – that is, tracts on the coast have a reduced number of neighbouring tracts, and so are less likely to show up as clusters. This might be expected to be the case for former fishing villages, many of which are poor communities, but isolated around the coast rather than clustered together as in inner-city areas. This in itself could be considered as a different form of spatial cluster, but one that could not be detected by LISA analysis. It should therefore be noted that the LISA maps are just one way to look at the changing geography of poverty, and they should be viewed in the context of the other evidence presented in this report, particularly the local area maps detailed in the section on 'Local case studies' (Chapter 7, page 49).

Table 12: High and low breadline poverty clusters occurring at every time period

	1970 households			1980 households			1990 households			2000 households		
	Total	Breadline poor	%	Total	Breadline poor	%	Total	Breadline poor	%	Total	Breadline poor	%
High breadline poverty clusters[a]												
Inner London	1,317,871	452,535	34.3	1,072,237	301,212	28.1	1,043,127	355,866	34.1	1,241,556	543,424	43.8
Central Birmingham	136,910	44,090	32.2	268,474	65,912	24.6	286,124	88,696	31.0	342,851	140,588	41.0
Inner Liverpool	196,348	66,274	33.8	199,684	53,832	27.0	224,065	75,294	33.6	263,533	108,454	41.2
Central Manchester	244,867	76,100	31.1	159,166	41,714	26.2	198,156	66,236	33.4	197,761	80,793	40.9
Urban South Yorkshire	125,124	37,835	30.2	90,167	22,585	25.0	108,351	36,084	33.3	108,892	44,634	41.0
Inner Tyneside	213,525	66,560	31.2	261,704	63,052	24.1	297,664	93,295	31.3	211,239	80,579	38.1
Much of Glasgow/Clyde	330,886	110,584	33.4	573,566	144,575	25.2	483,502	157,313	32.5	344,477	142,331	41.3
Low breadline poverty clusters[a]												
Central/Southern England	3,235,115	532,889	16.5	4,008,440	476,886	11.9	4,805,048	721,104	15.0	5,187,006	975,673	18.8
Rural North Yorkshire/Lancashire/Cumbria	44,203	8,792	19.9	238,905	29,002	12.1	346,414	54,802	15.8	281,378	55,424	19.7

Note: [a] Cluster names are for reference only, and refer to the contiguous set of tracts making up each cluster, rather than any formal or administrative boundary.

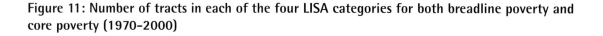

Figure 11: Number of tracts in each of the four LISA categories for both breadline poverty and core poverty (1970-2000)

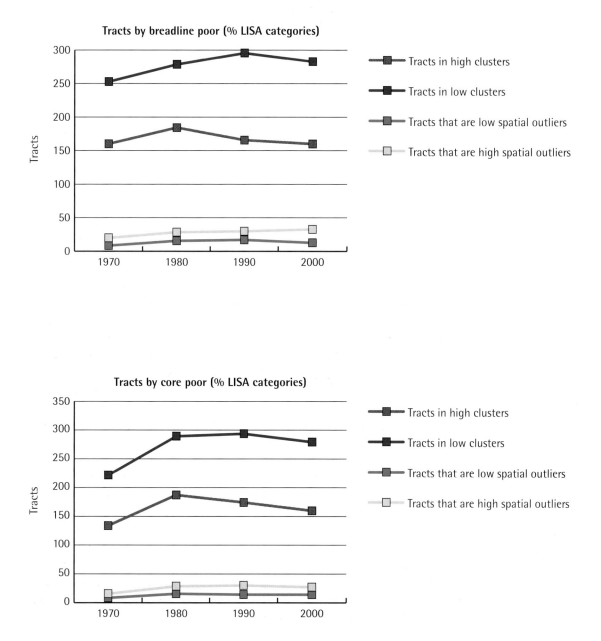

Wealth

Table 13 indicates a similar degree of spatial autocorrelation for the exclusive wealthy measure as for the poverty measures, around 0.5-0.6. This analysis of our entire geographical area suggests that during the 1980s, asset wealthy households became slightly less spatially concentrated, possibly reflecting the ripple of wealth outwards from London through the South East in response to increasing house prices. Then, during the late 1990s, the degree of spatial concentration increased again, with an increase in Moran's I from 0.55-0.60 over this relatively short period. The trend for the spatial concentration of the exclusive wealthy is similar, with the exception that Moran's I decreased substantially from 1980-90, then increasing to 1996 and again to 2000. This suggests that the exclusive wealthy became progressively more geographically concentrated from around 1990 onwards.

Table 13: Moran's I statistics for asset wealth and exclusive wealth measures[a]

	Asset wealthy	Exclusive wealthy
1980	0.5994	0.5616
1990	0.5575	0.3219
1996	0.5452	0.5517[b]
2000	0.6023	0.6014

Notes: [a]All *p*-values < 0.001; [b]The national exclusive wealthy proportion for 1996 was estimated as the mean of those for 1990 and 2000, and local estimates were derived using this proportion.

LISA were calculated as for the poverty data to investigate local spatial autocorrelation in more detail and to determine the locations of geographical clusters of high and low asset wealthy and exclusive wealthy rates (see Maps 8 and 9). The geography of clusters of high and low asset wealthy rates gets more distinct over time, becoming an increasingly clear north/south division by 2000. By this time, high levels of asset wealth are concentrated in southern England and parts of mid-Wales. There are two smaller high clusters in rural Cheshire and the surrounds of Harrogate. Clusters of low asset wealth are found in the south Wales Valleys, the West Midlands conurbation, the East End of London, the Potteries, parts of Merseyside, Lancashire, South Yorkshire, Humberside, urban north eastern England and in and around Glasgow. The spatial outliers also provide some interest, and are often found where they might be expected. For example, low rates of asset wealth in Great Yarmouth are proximal to high rates in surrounding Norfolk; high rates of asset wealthy in Edgbaston are found adjacent to low rates in surrounding parts of Birmingham.

The maps of spatial concentration for the exclusive wealthy measures also indicate an increasingly clear geography, in this case indicating by 2000 a 'core-periphery' pattern. During the two decades, exclusive wealthy households become more and more concentrated in an area spreading from the Cotswolds to west London and including much of the Home Counties. There are also two small clusters of high rates in rural Worcestershire and Cheshire. Low rates are clustered in an arc spreading around from the valleys of South Wales, West and North Wales, Liverpool, Manchester, South and West Yorkshire, Humberside, Lincolnshire and north Norfolk. Further small clusters of low rates are found in Cumbria, north east England and Glasgow.

Map 8: LISA for the % of households classified as asset wealthy at each time period

1980

1990

1996

2000

% asset wealthy households in tract

Little spatial autocorrelation
Cluster of areas with high wealth rates
Cluster of areas with low wealth rates
Low spatial outlier
High spatial outlier

Map 9: LISA for the % of households classified as exclusive wealthy at each time period

1980

1990

1996

2000

% exclusive wealthy households in tract

Little local spatial autocorrelation
Cluster of areas with high exclusive wealth rates
Cluster of areas with low exclusive wealth rates
Low spatial outlier
High spatial outlier

Segregation

The Index of Dissimilarity is a useful, simple measure for this kind of study, producing a summary measure of the relative segregation (or integration) of two groups across geographical areas. It effectively compares the distribution of the two groups, and calculates what proportion of one group would have to move (geographically) to result in an even distribution of both groups across all areas. The Index has commonly been used to investigate racial/ethnic segregation, but can equally be used to measure how segregated the poor – or wealthy – are from the rest of the population.

The 'symmetrical' version of the Index was calculated, for example, comparing the number of breadline poor households to the number of all other households. An index of 30% would indicate that 30% of poor households would need to move to create an even distribution of poor households across all areas. The more segregated and spatially concentrated a group is, the higher the Index of Dissimilarity.

The Index of Dissimilarity was calculated for each of the five groups in turn, so telling us at each time period what proportion of that group would have to move to result in an even distribution of the group across Britain. It measures each group against the remainder of groups considered together. The results are shown in Table 14 and Figure 12. Overall, we can see that the dissimilarity indices are substantially higher for the asset and exclusive wealthy households than the other three groups, indicating that these households are more segregated.

During the 1980s, while overall levels of asset wealthy households rose from 17% to 23% of households, the Index of Dissimilarity remained fairly constant at around 34-35%. Between 1990 and 2000 the national proportion of asset wealthy households stayed roughly the same, but the Index of Dissimilarity increased to 40%. The exclusive wealthy Index of Dissimilarity rose from 44 to 61% during the 1980s while the proportion of households classified as exclusive wealthy fell from 6.9 to 3.5%. Then, when this proportion rose back up to 5.6% in the 1990s, the exclusive wealthy Index of Dissimilarity stayed roughly the same at 60%.

As can be seen, in 1970 around 12% of core poor households would have to move to a different tract to create an even distribution of core poor households across all tracts. The core poor index then increased to around 15% in 1980, stayed about the same during the 1980s, and then fell slightly during the 1990s. The breadline poor index rose steadily across the 30-year period, from just under 15% in 1970 to over 18% in 2000.

Table 14: The Index of Dissimilarity for each measure at each time period

Dissimilarity indices	Time period (%)			
	1970	1980	1990	2000
Core poor	12.3	15.6	15.3	14.1
Breadline poor	14.7	16.7	17.1	18.3
Non-poor, non-wealthy		15.4	16.7	19.8
Asset wealthy		34.9	34.5	40.1
Exclusive wealthy		43.6	60.6	59.7

Figure 12: Dissimilarity indices for each of the five measures across all tracts in Britain across the study period

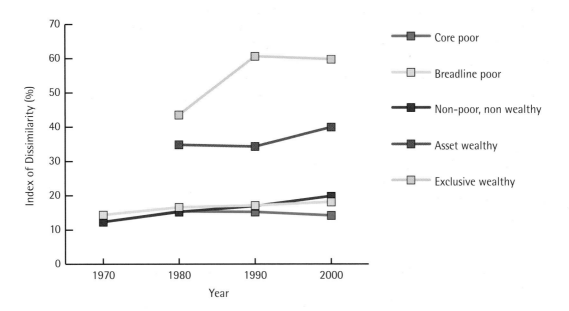

The 'middle' group of non-poor, non-wealthy households follows a similar trajectory to the core and breadline poor households, although here the index for these households rose slightly through the two decades, from 15% in 1980 to 20% in 2000.

In terms of the whole study period, the dissimilarity indices indicate that breadline poor, asset wealthy, exclusive wealthy and non-poor/non-wealthy households became more unevenly distributed, in agreement with the maps and findings of the polarisation and spatial concentration analyses above. The core poor became slightly more unevenly distributed during the 1970s, but this trend has been slowly reversing since 1980; these small changes are reflected in the little changing global spatial autocorrelation statistic (Moran's I) for core poverty described above.

Local issues

Locally sensitive poverty measures?

The models used to estimate the percentage of breadline poor and core poor households make the assumption that the weightings applied to census variables are appropriate for everywhere in Britain. For example, the model used with the 1991 Census estimates that 22% of the lone-parent households in every tract are breadline poor. The assumption that this percentage is similar in all areas is reasonable, but it is possible that locally sensitive models might produce more accurate estimates. In particular, it is often observed that London behaves differently to everywhere else in Britain in terms of social statistics and associations between them.

In order to begin to investigate this as a potential issue for future improvements to poverty (and wealth) models, we took a very simple approach. The relationship between each poverty index and its constituent census variables was assessed using correlation coefficients, separately for London and the remainder of Britain. While this is a somewhat circular analysis, it is still a useful means to start to gain an insight into geographical variations in the different measures used to estimate poverty.

The figures in Table 15 are correlation coefficients, which indicate the degree of association between each poverty index and the census variables used in its construction. These figures indicate that for most census variables, the association with the composite poverty index is similar for London tracts and tracts in the rest of Britain. However, there are some notable exceptions. The correlation between core poverty and percentage of two-pensioner households in 1970 is −0.40 in London, while it is +0.16 elsewhere. This suggests that the two-pensioner measure may not be a good indicator of core poverty in London. Similar differences are observed for the percentage of households with three or more children and poverty in 1980, and single-pensioner households and both poverty indices in 1990. There are no similar differentials between London and the rest of Britain for the 2000 indices.

These findings do not diminish the validity or appropriateness of the poverty indices, since the majority of the census component variables are strongly associated with the indices as would be expected, and the methodology used explicitly addresses issues of validity and reliability. However, it is possible that more complex methods (such as geographically weighted regression; see Fotheringham et al, 2002) could produce more locally sensitive poverty measures by allowing for spatial variation in the weightings attached to different indicator variables.

Table 15: The association between each poverty index and constituent census variables (correlation coefficients calculated separately for tracts in London and those in the rest of Britain)

Correlation with breadline poor	London	Rest of Britain	Correlation with core poor	London	Rest of Britain
1970			**1970**		
% sharing/lacking bath	0.93	0.69	% sharing/lacking bath	0.95	0.78
% no car	0.99	0.94	% no car	0.97	0.86
% social renting	0.31	0.39	% private renting	0.87	0.58
% private renting	0.83	0.39	% low socioeconomic group	0.54	0.59
% low socioeconomic group	0.60	0.64	% single pensioner	0.81	0.66
% overcrowded	0.85	0.56	% two pensioners	-0.40	0.16
% single pensioner	0.81	0.52			
% two pensioners	-0.40	-0.03			
1980			**1980**		
% sharing household amenities	0.71	0.35	% sharing household amenities	0.49	0.21
% sharing dwelling	0.63	0.20	% no car	0.95	0.88
% no car	0.98	0.92	% social renting	0.90	0.86
% social renting	0.75	0.80	% unemployed	0.97	0.88
% private renting	0.53	0.05	% lone parent	0.84	0.75
% unemployed	0.94	0.85	% 3+ children	0.08	0.34
% 3+ children	-0.12	0.22			
1990			**1990**		
% lone parent	0.86	0.88	% lone parent	0.88	0.89
% unskilled	0.58	0.60	% unskilled	0.62	0.62
% home not owned	0.98	0.92	% home not owned	0.96	0.90
% no car	0.99	0.97	% no car	0.98	0.97
% 3+ children	0.28	0.34	% 3+ children	0.33	0.37
% unemployed	0.86	0.89	% unemployed	0.90	0.91
% single pensioner	-0.01	0.31	% single pensioner	-0.06	0.30
2000			**2000**		
% overcrowded	0.79	0.66	% overcrowded	0.77	0.65
% social renting	0.94	0.91	% social renting	0.95	0.91
% lone parent	0.74	0.88	% lone parent	0.75	0.88
% unemployed	0.95	0.90	% unemployed	0.95	0.90
% no car	0.93	0.95	% no car	0.92	0.95
% private renting	0.30	0.17	% private renting	0.27	0.16
% long-term illness	0.40	0.71	% long-term illness	0.41	0.73
% sharing amenities	0.44	0.51	% sharing amenities	0.42	0.49
% low social class	0.77	0.86			

Local case studies

In this section, we present a set of time series maps illustrating in more detail the changing geography of poverty and wealth in a selection of British regions and cities. The intention here is not to present an atlas of all areas, but to highlight some local stories that help us to understand the national analysis presented above. The areas are discussed in the order in which the maps appear in Maps 10-23 below. Data are available to allow interested readers to investigate further any specific areas of interest (see www.sasi.group.shef.ac.uk/research/transformation).

In central Glasgow, reasonably high breadline poverty levels decline slightly during the 1970s, but then increase through the 1980s and 1990s. By 2000, seven tracts in the city have more than half of their households in breadline poverty (see Map 10). In Map 11, we can see that the asset wealthy time series is very consistent for the Glasgow area. Most of the city's tracts have less than 10% asset wealthy households at every time period, with only the more rural tracts to the north and south showing higher rates.

Moving south to Yorkshire (Map 12), with the major cities of Leeds, Bradford and York, a similar pattern in terms of increasing urban poverty over the decades is apparent. The year 2000 map in particular highlights the common feature of many British cities in having their poorest neighbourhoods towards the east. The low prevalence of asset wealthy in Leeds/ Bradford becomes clearer and more contiguous as time progresses, as do the increasing levels of asset wealthy in tracts closer to (but not in) the city of York, and in and around Harrogate (see Map 13).

The maps of the Liverpool/Manchester area, shown in Maps 14 and 15, also support our previous assertions that the highest levels of spatial concentration of wealth in this time series were in 2000. The lowest rates become concentrated in the two major cities, while higher rates become more clustered in rural areas of Cheshire (around Macclesfield) and Lancashire (around Chorley). Breadline poverty patterns across the decades here are again familiar, by 2000 becoming very obviously gradated out from the central areas of both Merseyside (Birkenhead North-East, Liverpool Riverside and West Derby West tracts) and Manchester (Ardwick tract).

The typical urban poverty patterns are repeated in the West Midlands conurbation, with four tracts in central Birmingham having rates of more than 50% by 2000 – Ladywood West and East, Hodge Hill West and Sparkbrook (see Map 16). The asset wealthy geography here indicates polarisation over the two decades, with an increasingly marked distinction between low rates in the central urban area and higher rates in outlying tracts, particularly to the south of Birmingham (Map 17). By 2000, the percentage of households classified as asset wealthy in the four tracts mentioned above are 4.0%, 1.1%, 1.0% and 0.5% respectively.

When compared to the very high levels of breadline poverty in these urban areas, the maps of South Wales (Map 18) show relatively low levels given the general assumption that the ex-coal mining valleys have been some of the poorest parts of Britain over this time period. However, by 2000, the Valleys do have breadline poverty rates of around 30-40%, as do the more industrial areas of Swansea, Neath, Port Talbot, Cardiff and Newport. The asset wealthy maps shown in Map 19 are almost the inverse of those of breadline poverty, highlighting the juxtaposition of the Valleys with the much more wealthy areas of Monmouthshire, the Gower and the outskirts of Cardiff.

The maps of London very clearly demonstrate the development of an increasingly intense 'bulls-eye' effect, with 15 tracts in 2000 having breadline poverty rates greater than 50% (see Map 20). The maps of asset wealthy for London (Map 21) again demonstrate a very clear polarisation over the 20-year period, resulting in a clear gradation from low asset wealthy in the East End to higher levels in the west of the city. Finally, the wider maps of the Home Counties (Maps 22 and 23) show how these changing circumstances in the capital continue to its surrounding areas. The consistently low levels of poverty and high concentration of wealth in the Home Counties are striking, with only an occasional anomaly, such as Crawley in 2000, disrupting the pattern.

Viewed in combination, these local maps give greater insight into the national maps of non-poor, non-wealthy households presented in the section on 'Non-poor, non-wealthy' (Chapter 5, page 25), where we see the gradual disappearance of the non-poor, non-wealthy 'middle' households from London and the South East.

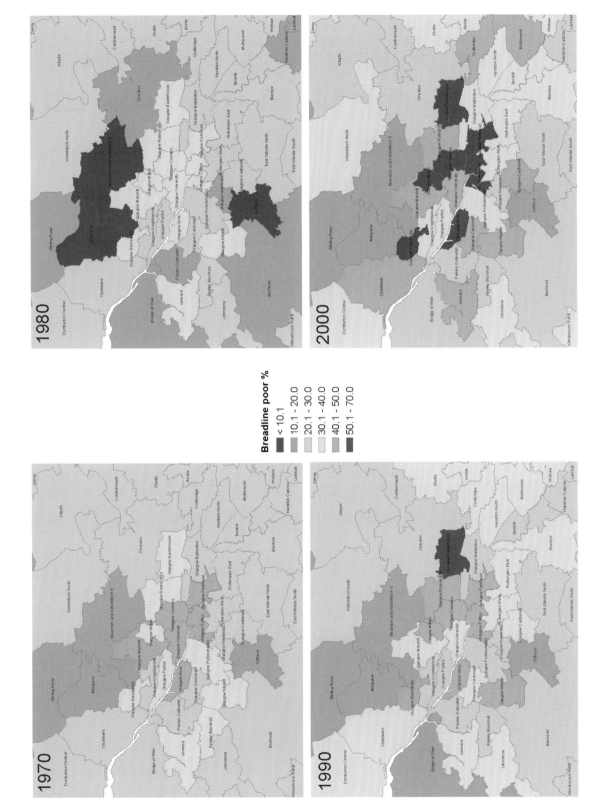

Map 10: Breadline poor households across the Glasgow area (1970–2000)

Breadline poor %

< 10.1
10.1 - 20.0
20.1 - 30.0
30.1 - 40.0
40.1 - 50.0
50.1 - 70.0

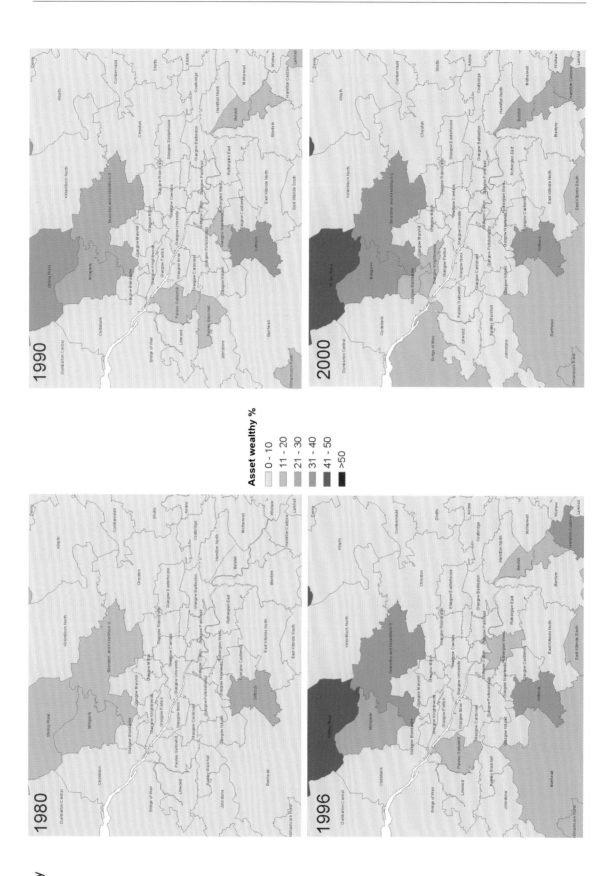

Map 11: Asset wealthy households across the Glasgow area (1980–2000)

Asset wealthy %

0 - 10
11 - 20
21 - 30
31 - 40
41 - 50
>50

Map 12: Breadline poor
households across the
Yorkshire area
(1970–2000)

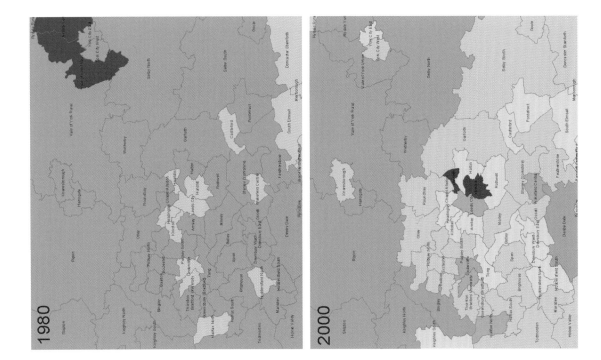

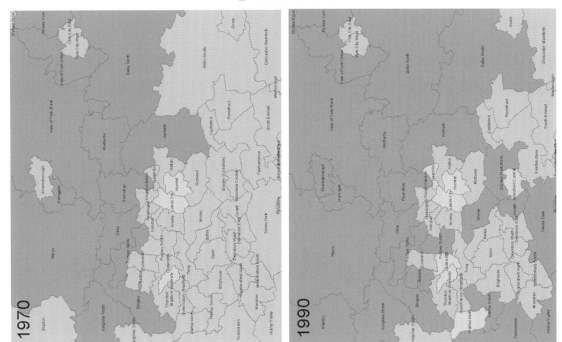

Breadline poor %

- < 10.1
- 10.1 - 20.0
- 20.1 - 30.0
- 30.1 - 40.0
- 40.1 - 50.0
- 50.1 - 70.0

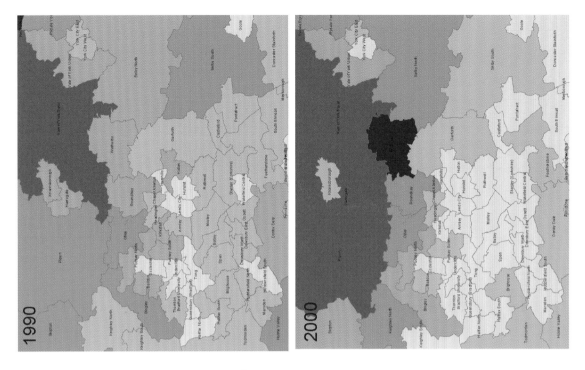

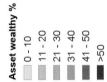

Asset wealthy %

0 - 10
11 - 20
21 - 30
31 - 40
41 - 50
>50

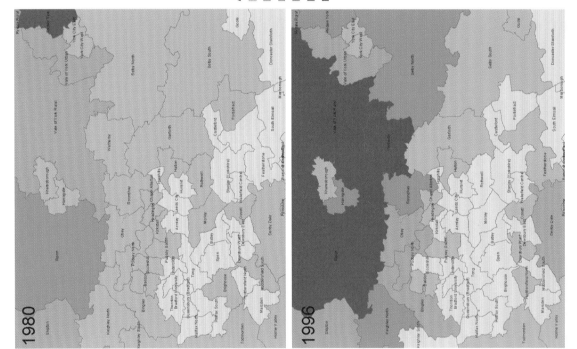

Map 13: Asset wealthy
households across
the Yorkshire area
(1980–2000)

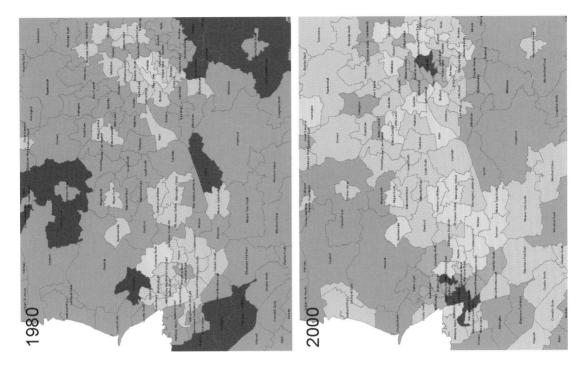

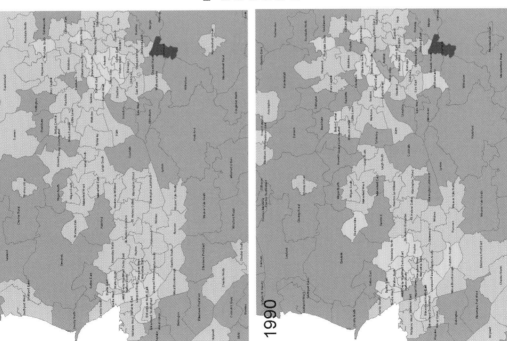

Map 14: Breadline poor households across the Liverpool/ Manchester area (1970–2000)

Breadline poor %

< 10.1
10.1 - 20.0
20.1 - 30.0
30.1 - 40.0
40.1 - 50.0
50.1 - 70.0

1970

1990

1980

2000

TO36985

Asset wealthy %

0 - 10
11 - 20
21 - 30
31 - 40
41 - 50
>50

Map 15: Asset wealthy
households across the
Liverpool/Manchester
area (1980-2000)

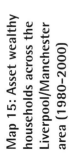

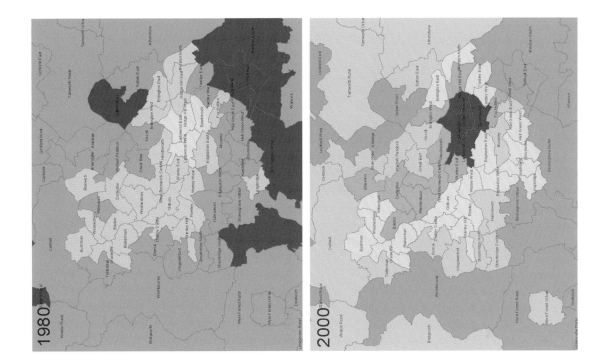

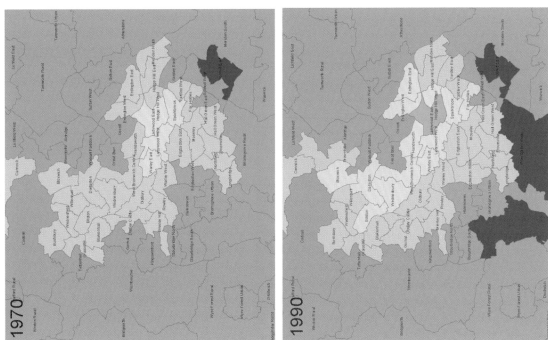

Map 16: Breadline poor households across the West Midlands conurbation (1970–2000)

Breadline poor %

< 10.1

10.1 - 20.0

20.1 - 30.0

30.1 - 40.0

40.1 - 50.0

50.1 - 70.0

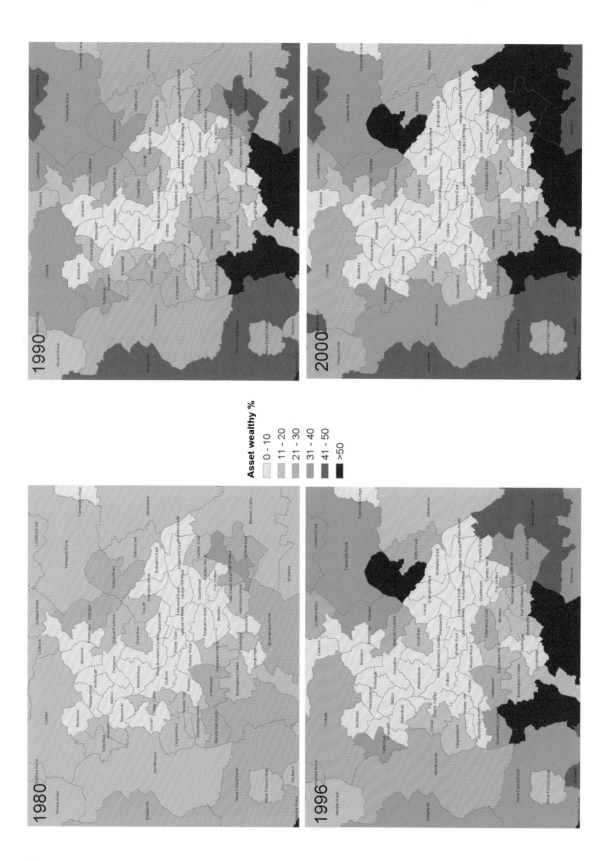

Asset wealthy %

0 – 10
11 – 20
21 – 30
31 – 40
41 – 50
>50

Map 17: Asset wealthy households across the West Midlands conurbation (1980–2000)

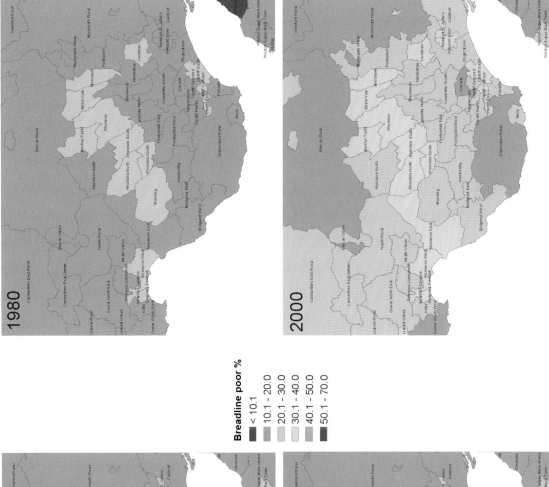

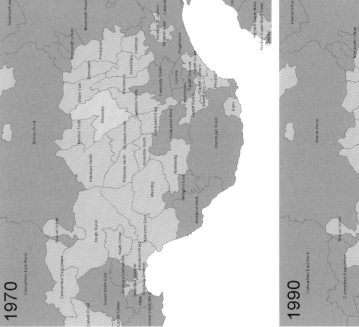

Map 18: Breadline poor households across South Wales (1970–2000)

Breadline poor %

< 10.1
10.1 – 20.0
20.1 – 30.0
30.1 – 40.0
40.1 – 50.0
50.1 – 70.0

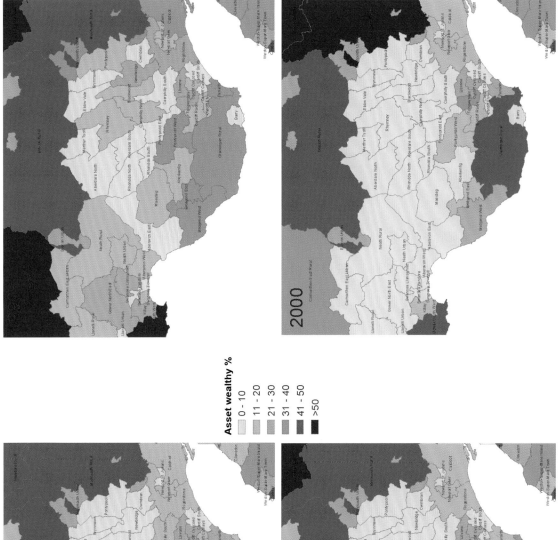

Asset wealthy %

0 - 10
11 - 20
21 - 30
31 - 40
41 - 50
>50

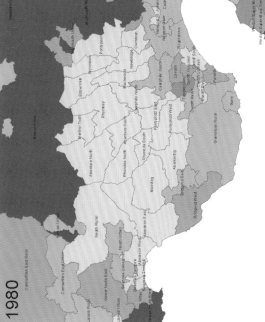

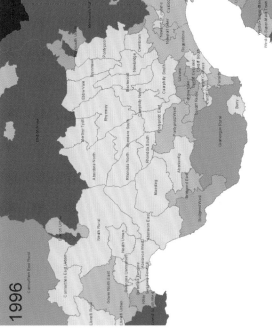

Map 19: Asset wealthy households across South Wales (1980–2000)

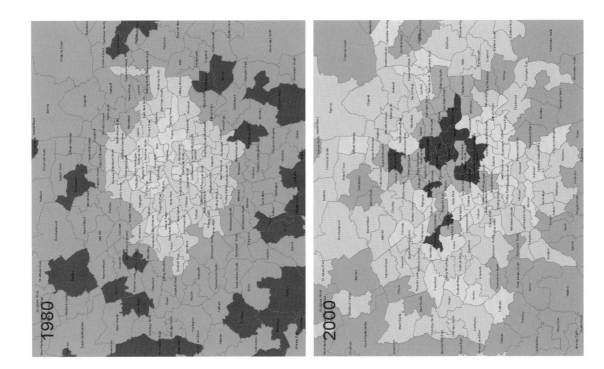

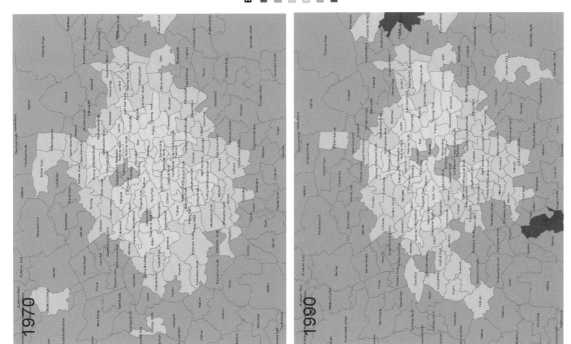

Map 20: Breadline
poor households across
London (1970–2000)

Breadline poor %

< 10.1
10.1 – 20.0
20.1 – 30.0
30.1 – 40.0
40.1 – 50.0
50.1 – 70.0

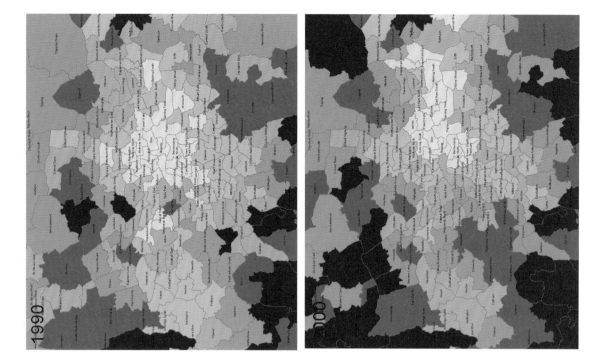

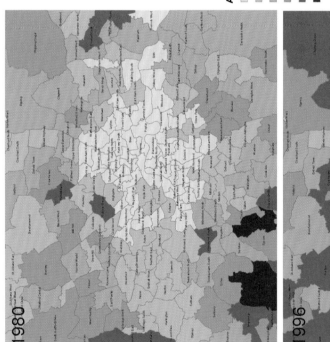

Asset wealthy %

0 – 10
11 – 20
21 – 30
31 – 40
41 – 50
>50

Map 21: Asset wealthy
households across London
(1980–2000)

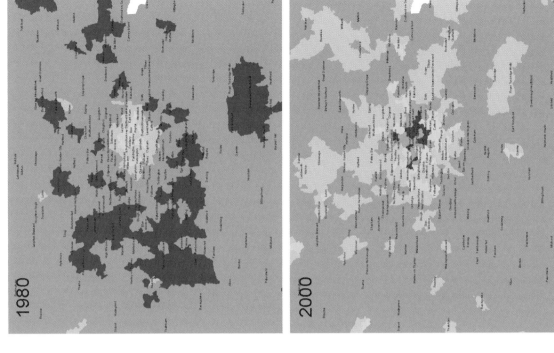

Map 22: Breadline
poor households across
the Home Counties
(including London)
(1970–2000)

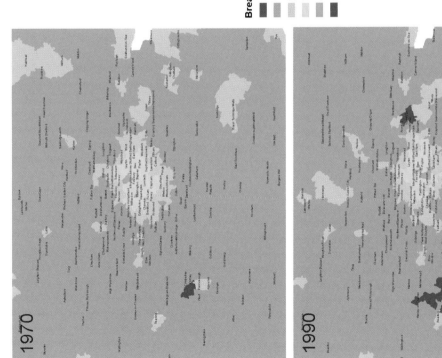

Breadline poor %

< 10.1
10.1 – 20.0
20.1 – 30.0
30.1 – 40.0
40.1 – 50.0
50.1 – 70.0

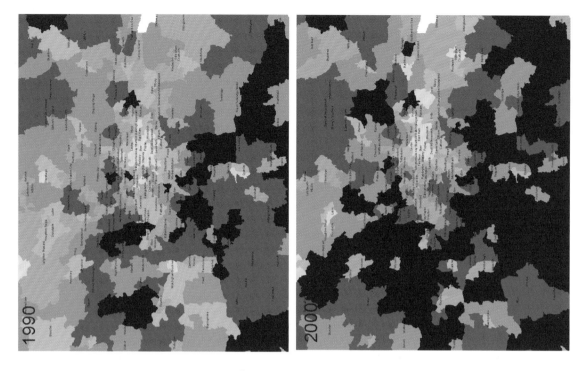

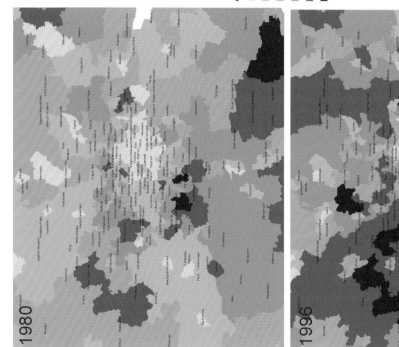

Asset wealthy %

0 - 10
11 - 20
21 - 30
31 - 40
41 - 50
>50

Map 23: Asset wealthy households across the Home Counties (including London) (1980–2000)

8

What has happened since 2000?

Since the next census will not be taken until 2011, it will be some time before the time series of wealth and poverty geography presented here can be extended beyond 2000. However, we have undertaken an analysis of data that are available for more recent years, which may give us an indication of the direction in which this decade is progressing. Ideally we would be able to compare poverty- and wealth-related datasets from around 2000 and 2005/06 to gain an insight into the changing patterns of inequality in the first half of this decade. The ability to carry out this analysis is determined by the data that are available, so in some cases we have only been able to look at change over a shorter period of time since the turn of the millennium.

Given that there are no specific 'poverty' or 'wealth' datasets for this time period, we have used modern equivalents of Beveridge's five 'Giant Evils' (Beveridge, 1942): Want (we have looked at income); Ignorance (higher education participation); Idleness (JSA claimants); Squalor (asset wealth and lack of asset wealth); and Disease (Incapacity Benefit claimants) as a framework for this section of analysis. For each of the five, we have selected a relevant contemporary issue, updating the language and concepts from the 1940s. We have then used a relevant dataset to compare the most recent data to that for around the year 2000 for each issue. Some of the subjects we investigate here are poverty related (such as benefits claimants), while some are more wealth orientated (such as housing wealth).

Income

In recent years, a subsidiary of Barclays Bank scans the records each year of the bank accounts of customers and estimates annual income based on regular payments into those accounts. This is a novel measure of income and in many cases will be more accurate than that which the customers report to the Inland Revenue, tell their spouses or even know themselves. It does suffer from some limitations, for example, it is an estimate for bank accounts, some of which may be joint accounts. In addition, this measure excludes poorer groups who may be financially excluded and do not hold any bank accounts. Also if a large number of, say, students open up bank accounts in an area in a particular year, average incomes may appear to fall. It is also only a sample from one bank (which does not report for Scotland) – nevertheless it is up to date and very interesting data, providing unique insight into the spatial distribution of income, given that there are no national official sources of income data.

Map 24 shows this average income for parliamentary constituencies (these data are not available for tracts) across England and Wales in 2005. As might be expected, this map shows that the highest incomes are to be found in the periphery of London, along with some more rural parts of northern England. Map 25 shows the change in this average income figure from 2003-05, and Figure 13 plots 2003 income against change since 2003. The charts clearly show that those constituencies with the highest average income in 2003 had the greatest increase during the two years to 2005, while the areas with the lowest incomes in 2003 were most likely to see the greatest declines in income over the same period. This is the case for both absolute and relative/percentage change. The correlation coefficients for these scatter plots are 0.61, *p*<0.001 (absolute change) and 0.59, *p*<0.001 (percentage change).

Map 24: Average income to bank accounts by parliamentary constituency (2005)

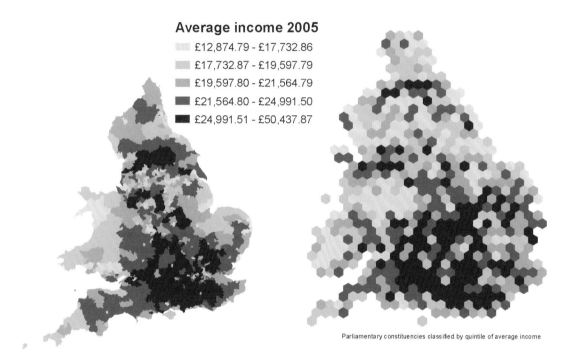

Parliamentary constituencies classified by quintile of average income

Map 25: Change in average income to bank accounts by parliamentary constituency from 2003–05

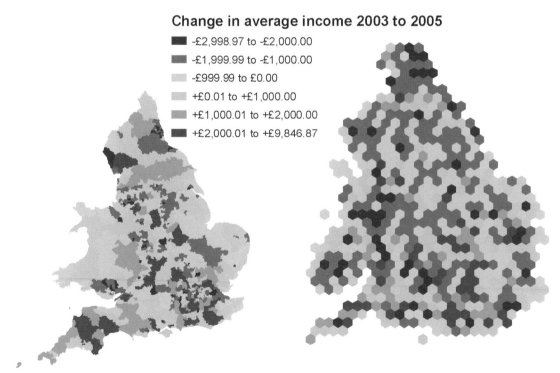

Figure 13: Scatter plot of constituency average income (2003) against absolute (£) and relative (%) change in income (2003-05)

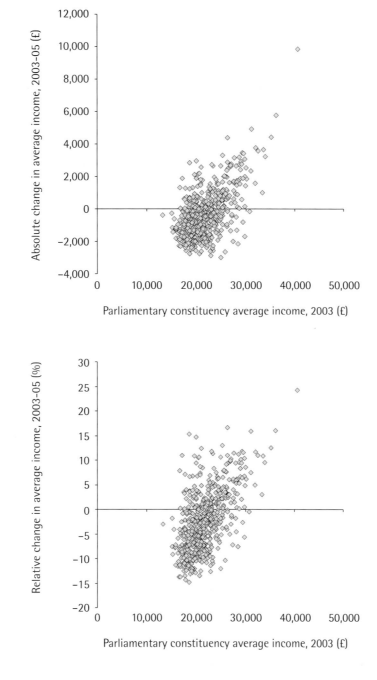

While income is not the same as wealth, in terms of 'Want', the income data here give a good indication of the ability of local populations to purchase goods and services, whether luxury or essential. This analysis suggests that at the start of this decade, those populations with the highest incomes were likely to experience the greatest increases in those incomes. Conversely, populations with the lowest incomes were most likely to see a decline in their incomes.

An analysis of the spatial concentration of change in income from 2003-05 (analogous to that discussed in Chapter 6) produced Map 26. This shows geographical clusters of high percentage increases in income around London, the south west of England, rural central southern England and north Yorkshire. The geographical clusters of low (that is, negative) income change are in South Wales, the urban West Midlands, northern cities and the north east of England.

Map 26: Spatial concentration analysis of the change in income between 2003 and 2005 for parliamentary constituencies

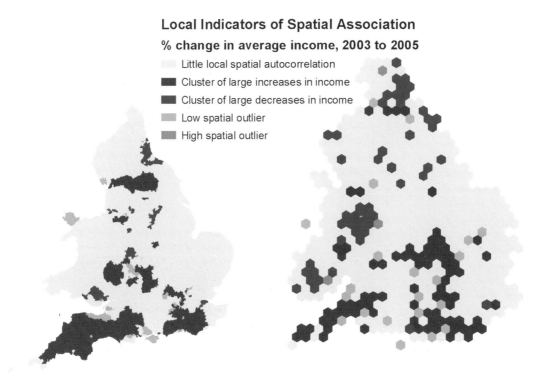

Local Indicators of Spatial Association

% change in average income, 2003 to 2005

Little local spatial autocorrelation
Cluster of large increases in income
Cluster of large decreases in income
Low spatial outlier
High spatial outlier

If the assumption is made that these trends and geographical patterns in income are indicative of the progression of wealth and poverty during the first decade of the millennium, it would suggest that the patterns observed during the 1980s and 1990s are likely to continue.

Lastly, the breadline poverty indicator for 2000 was recalculated for constituencies, and these were used to chart the change in average income by poverty decile. The graphs in Figure 14 indicate that the greatest income increases were in the least poor constituencies, while the poorer constituencies tended to experience quite substantial decreases in average income. The patterns are very similar, whether considering absolute or proportional change over the two-year period.

Figure 14: Change in constituency average income (2003–05) by breadline poverty decile (2000)

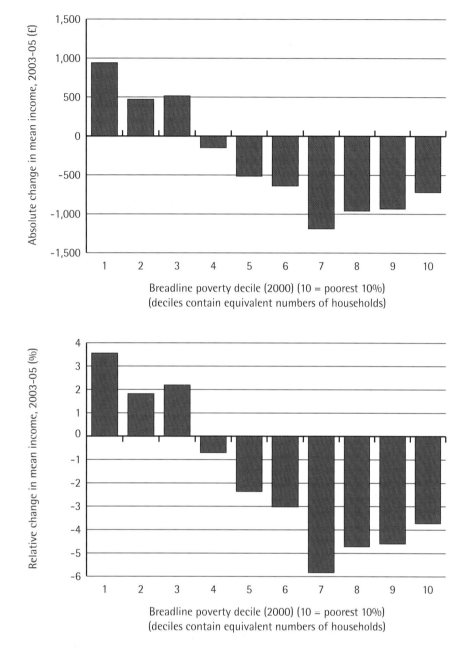

Breadline poverty decile (2000) (10 = poorest 10%)
(deciles contain equivalent numbers of households)

Education

Data on the proportion of young people entering higher education (HE) across Britain were obtained from the Higher Education Funding Council for England (HEFCE). Figures were available for the relevant age cohorts of young people, the first eligible to graduate between 1997 and 2001 (entering HE 1994-96) and the second graduating 2001-05 (entering between 1998 and 2000).

Map 27 shows the distribution of HE participation rates for the first cohort, exiting 1997-2001. While there is no clearly defined geographical pattern, it does appear that the highest participation rates – and those areas achieving the target 50% – are mostly around west London, a few parts of rural northern England, and Central Scotland. Low participation rates, under 20%, are largely to be found in the post-industrial areas of the north and midlands of England and the valleys of South Wales, along with east London and south coast cities such as Portsmouth, Southampton and Plymouth. This is an interesting finding that may be worth exploring further, given the presence of large universities in these areas.

Map 27: Higher Education participation (1997–2001 exit cohort)

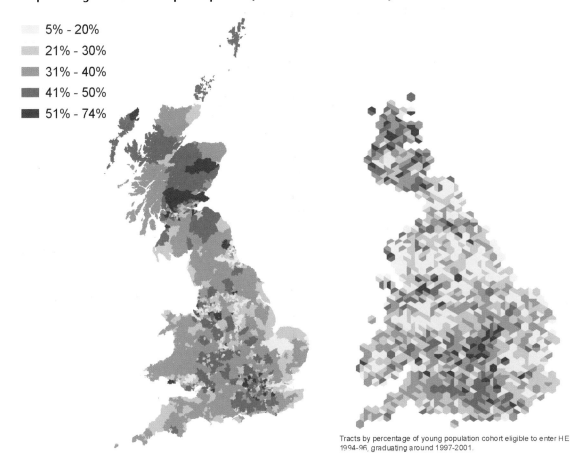

5% - 20%
21% - 30%
31% - 40%
41% - 50%
51% - 74%

Tracts by percentage of young population cohort eligible to enter HE 1994-96, graduating around 1997-2001.

In order to investigate change between the two periods, the tracts were divided into deciles of participation rates for both cohorts combined, weighted by cohort size to ensure that each decile contained roughly similar numbers of potential entrants. The graphs in Figure 15 show the absolute and proportional change in total participation rates for these tracts by decile, between the first and second cohorts. The first graph shows that absolute increases in participation rates were quite low and similar – around one percentage point – for the lowest and highest deciles, and increases were smaller for the middle deciles. In proportional terms, given that initial rates were substantially lower in the bottom deciles (by definition), the second graph indicates that the largest proportional increases occurred in those tracts with the lowest overall rates. This would suggest that attempts to disproportionately increase HE participation among populations with the lowest rates have been successful, to some extent, although absolute increases were similar for tracts with the highest participation.[10]

Figure 16 also indicates that attempts to 'widen participation' in the poorest areas of Britain appear to have been somewhat successful. This shows that participation rates increased the most, in both absolute and proportional terms, among young people living in areas with the highest poverty rates, where rates increased from around 17-20% from one cohort to the next. The rate among tracts in the highest decile remained static at around 42%. This pattern has been investigated further, and it has been suggested that the rising participation observed for poor areas is largely explained by increases in London, and by increases among black and minority ethnic populations (Corver, 2005; personal communication 2006).

---

[10] These findings are largely in agreement with those of a 2005 HEFCE report (Corver, 2005); relevant parts of the HEFCE report are discussed in Appendix 1.

Figure 15: Change in HE participation rates between 1997/2001 and 2001/05 exit cohorts, by decile of participation rate for both cohorts combined

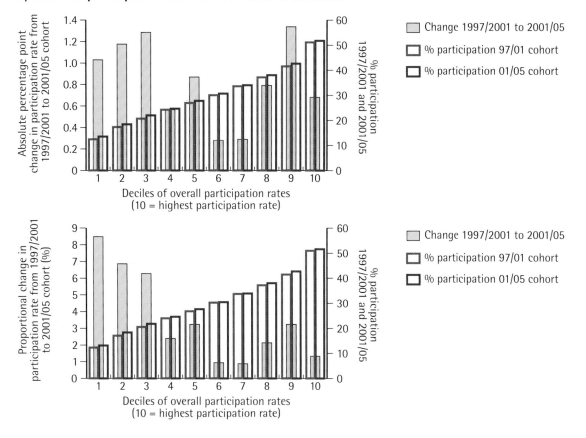

Figure 16: Change in HE participation rates between 1997/2001 and 2001/05 cohorts, by decile of percentage of poor households (2001)

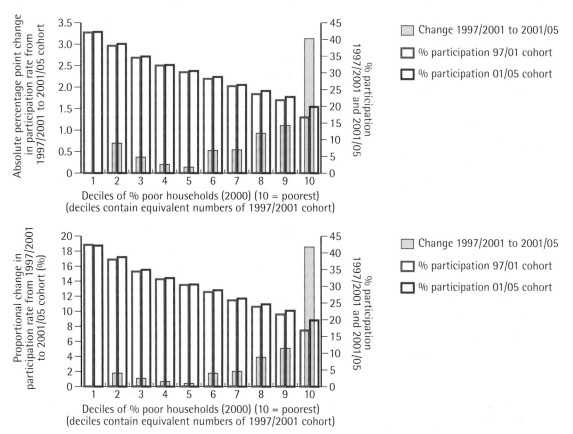

Unemployment

The Work and Pensions Longitudinal Study (WPLS), carried out by the Department for Work and Pensions, produces census (100%) counts of working-age benefit claimants for small areas across Britain (DWP, 2005). These counts were obtained for August 2000 and August 2005, and aggregated to tracts, to investigate any changes in the geographical distribution of Jobseeker's Allowance (JSA) claimants over the first half of the decade. The denominator used to calculate the proportion of the population claiming JSA in 2000 was the 2001 Census count of the working-age population, using the same definition of working age as the WPLS (men aged 16-64 and women aged 16-59). Since there are no small area population estimates available for 2005, we have used the 2001 and 2005 parliamentary constituency electorates to adjust the 2001 Census counts, producing estimated tract-level denominators for 2005 JSA claimants.[11]

Map 28 shows high JSA claimant levels in 2000 to be found where they might be expected. High percentages are seen in inner-city areas, especially London and the north of England, deindustrialised areas (such as mining – South Wales and northern England, and fishing – coastal areas, especially south west and eastern England), and remote rural parts of

Map 28: Geographical distribution of JSA claimants (August 2000)

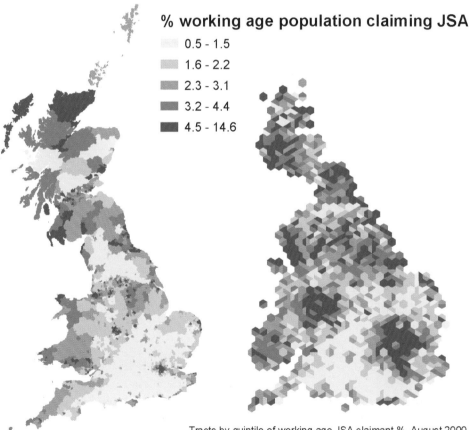

% working age population claiming JSA

- 0.5 - 1.5
- 1.6 - 2.2
- 2.3 - 3.1
- 3.2 - 4.4
- 4.5 - 14.6

Tracts by quintile of working age JSA claimant %, August 2000

---

[11] Since Scottish constituencies changed substantially between 2001 and 2005, we have been unable to adjust the denominators for Scotland on a local basis. The 2001 Census counts for all Scottish tracts were therefore adjusted using the rate of change in electorate for the whole of Scotland (–3.6%).

Britain. It is noteworthy that the geographical patterns shown here are in general similar to those identified by Palmer et al (2006), who investigated the geographical distribution of the recipients of a wide range of benefits at census super output area level in Britain. Map 29 shows the change in JSA claimants over the five years to 2005, and interestingly indicates that the highest proportional decreases in claimant levels are observed in areas with some of the highest levels in the previous map. However some of these decreases in JSA claimant levels may be due to displacement to Incapacity Benefit (IB).

Map 29: Geographical distribution of change in JSA claimants (2000-05)

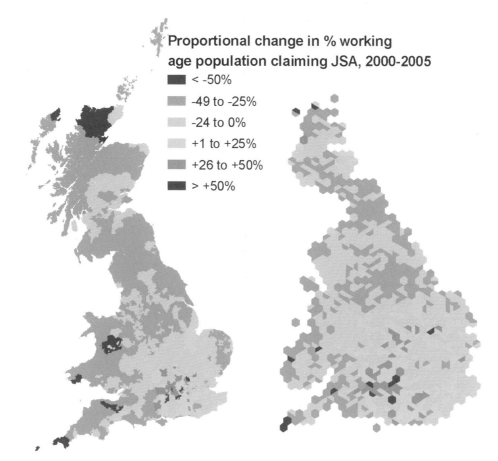

This trend is confirmed by the graphs in Figure 17, which indicate that the highest declines in JSA claimant levels between 2000 and 2005 have been in those areas in the highest deciles of claimant rates (deciles based on both periods combined). Similar charts in Figure 18 indicate that the largest absolute declines in the percentage of working-age people claiming JSA have occurred in the poorest tracts according to the 2000 breadline poverty measure. However, the trend across poverty deciles of proportional change in JSA claimant levels is not quite so clear, although it is indicative of relatively large decreases in the poorest decile of areas.

Figure 17: Absolute and proportional change in tract JSA claimant percentages (2000–05), by JSA claimant % decile for 2000/05

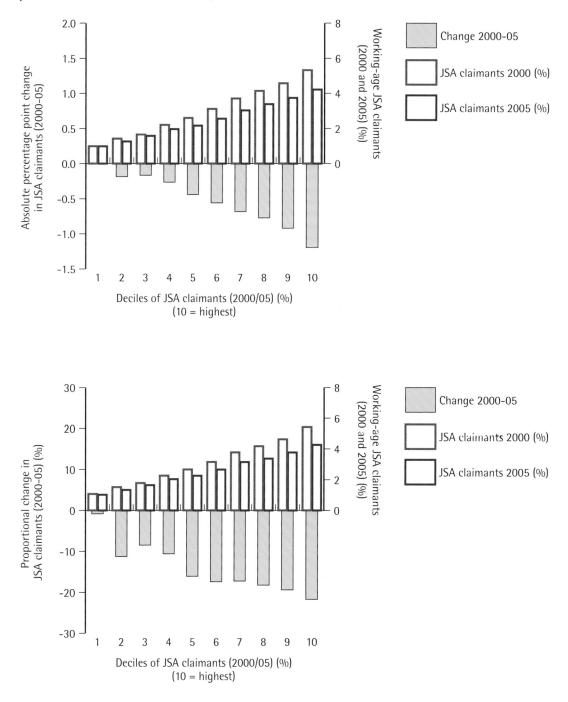

The spatial concentration analysis depicted in Map 30 adds weight to this analysis, and indicates geographical clustering of increasing JSA claimant levels in the south east of England (outside of London), some parts of the urban West Midlands, and Port Glasgow/ Greenock. Large clusters of decreasing levels are indicated in south west England, Wales, northern England and rural Scotland. These trends would suggest a move toward greater equality during the first half of this decade, with JSA claimant levels falling most in areas with the highest levels, and conversely some increases in claimant numbers in areas with

Figure 18: Absolute and proportional change in tract JSA claimant percentages (2000-05), by breadline poverty decile (2000)

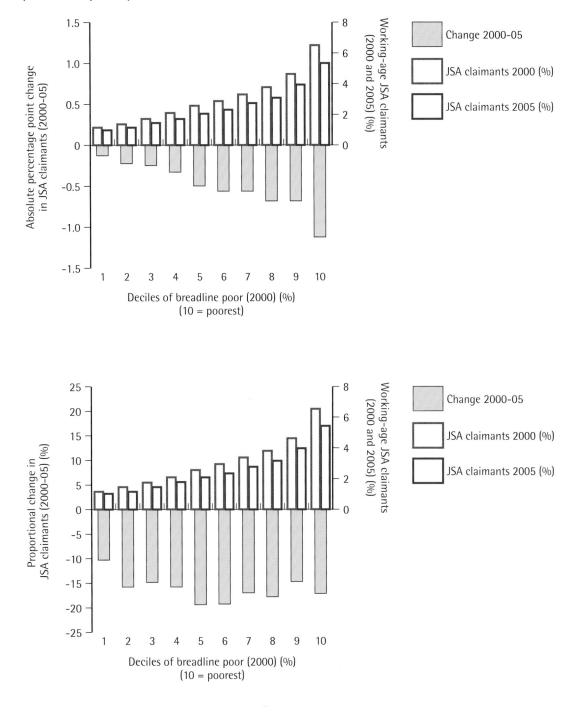

very low levels in 2000. There are, however, some places bucking this trend – those with relatively high levels in 2000 experiencing an increase over the five years. These areas include Handsworth, Hodge Hill West and Ladywood East (all in Birmingham). It should also be noted that in some cases the reduction in JSA claimant levels might be due to people leaving the labour market and becoming economically inactive, especially as seen in some formerly unpopular social housing estates in recent years (for instance, see Tunstall and Coulter, 2006).

Map 30: Spatial concentration analysis of the change in % of the working-age population claiming JSA (2000-05)

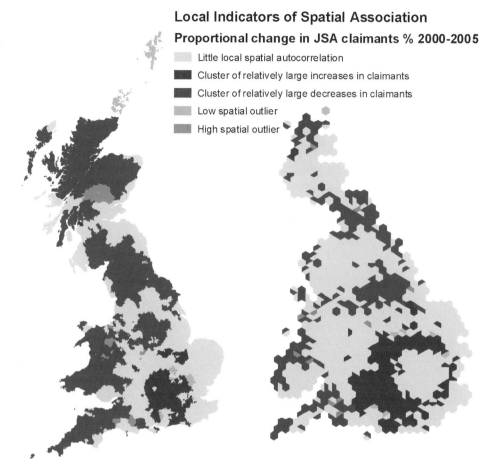

Local Indicators of Spatial Association

Proportional change in JSA claimants % 2000-2005

- Little local spatial autocorrelation
- Cluster of relatively large increases in claimants
- Cluster of relatively large decreases in claimants
- Low spatial outlier
- High spatial outlier

Wealth

The housing wealth data used to construct the asset wealth measures described in the section 'Wealth' (Chapter 3, page 12) included data up to 2003. In order to investigate changes in wealth at the beginning of the 21st century, we estimated the number of asset wealthy households in 2002 and 2003. These figures could then be added to the series described in the main section of analysis. The Inheritance Tax and housing wealth thresholds used for these years are listed in Table 16.

Table 16: Thresholds used for estimation of asset wealthy households (2002 and 2003)

Year	Inheritance Tax threshold (£)	Housing wealth as a percentage of total wealth[a]	Housing wealth threshold (£)
2002	250,000	42.0	105,000
2003	255,000	41.7	106,335

Note: [a] Non-financial assets less loans secured on dwellings as a proportion of total assets.

Source: National Statistics (2006c), table 5.22

Figure 19 shows the change in the national percentage of asset wealthy households from 1983-2003. This shows a clear overall increase from 1999-2002, and again to 2003.

Figure 19: Change in % of asset wealthy households from 1983–2003

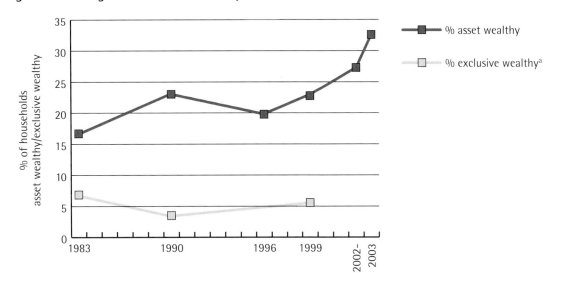

Note: [a] See Appendix 1 for variability around the exclusive wealthy estimate and its trend. Exclusive wealthy figures for 2002 and 2003 were not available.

Map 31 continues the sequence of maps of asset wealthy households presented in the section on 'Wealth' (Chapter 5, page 22), while Map 32 shows the change in the percentage of households classified as wealthy from 1999-2003. These maps indicate increases in numbers of asset wealthy households in much of the country, but with declines notable in small pockets of Scotland, south Wales, towns and cities of the north and Midlands and London.

Map 31: Percentage of asset wealthy households (2003), based on housing wealth data

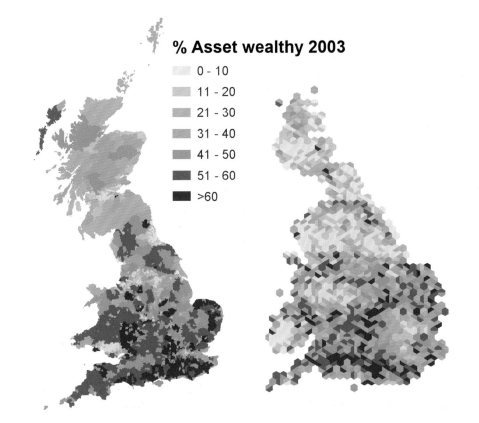

Map 32: Change in % of asset wealthy households between 1999 and 2003

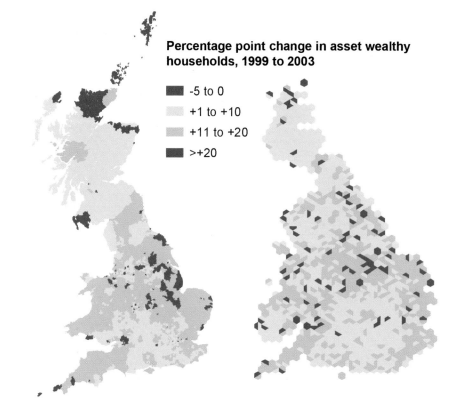

Percentage point change in asset wealthy households, 1999 to 2003

- ■ -5 to 0
- ▢ +1 to +10
- ▨ +11 to +20
- ■ >+20

The graphs in Figure 20 suggest that from 1999-2003, in general, areas with higher proportions of wealthy households experienced greater absolute increases. However, these absolute increases give rise to greater proportional increases in the tracts with initially lower rates. For example, while those tracts in decile one experienced an increase from just 1.9% to 3.8% asset wealthy households, this equates to a 100% proportional increase. Conversely, in decile ten, the increase from 53% to 62% asset wealthy households equates to a proportional increase of just 17%. Despite the encouraging gradient in terms of proportional change, the existing magnitude of the variation in wealth across areas is such that this process would take a very long time to bring about equality. In fact, it is far more likely that Inheritance Tax thresholds will be raised again, and inequalities rise, than we eventually see all households in every tract eligible to be classified as 'asset wealthy' according to this measure.

Figure 20: Percentage point and proportional change in asset wealthy households from 1999–2005

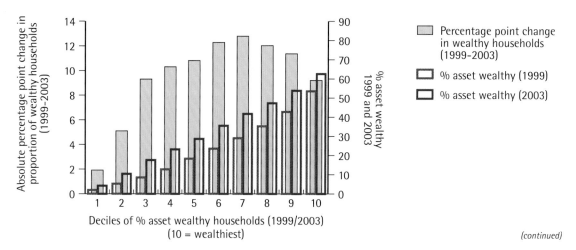

Legend:
- ▨ Percentage point change in wealthy households (1999-2003)
- ▢ % asset wealthy (1999)
- ▢ % asset wealthy (2003)

x-axis: Deciles of % asset wealthy households (1999/2003) (10 = wealthiest)

left y-axis: Absolute percentage point change in proportion of wealthy households (1999-2003)

right y-axis: % asset wealthy 1999 and 2003

(continued)

Figure 20: (continued)

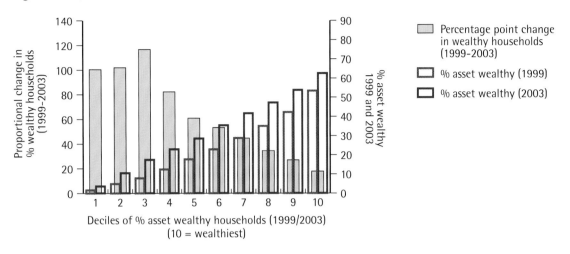

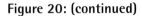

Map 33 shows the spatial concentration (LISA) analysis of the change in asset wealthy households between 1999 and 2003. The clusters of low values (that is, decreases or low absolute increases in asset wealthy) are found across Scotland, towns and cities in the north and midlands of England, the south Wales valleys, London and around Bournemouth. Spatial clusters of high values (large increases) are quite widespread, from Devon and Cornwall, west Wales, East Anglia and the north and east midlands of England.

Map 33: Spatial concentration analysis of the change in asset wealthy households % between 1999 and 2003

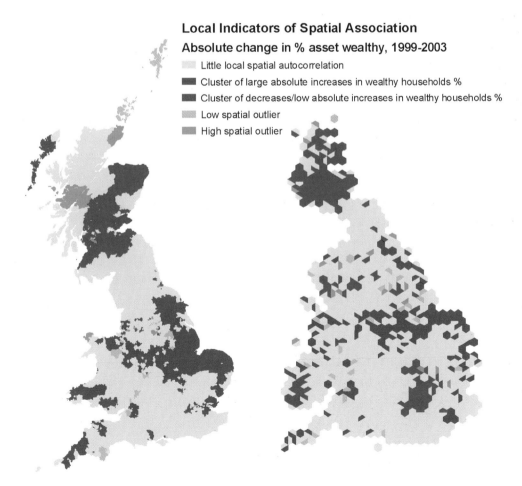

The graph of polarisation in Figure 21 indicates a trend of polarisation over this time period, continuing that of the late 1990s (see the section on 'Polarisation', Chapter 6, page 28), where the population living in tracts with high asset wealthy rates (category 14) increased, while the population in areas with few wealthy households (category 1) decreased.

Figure 21: Spatial polarisation of the population by tract asset wealthy density (1999–2003)

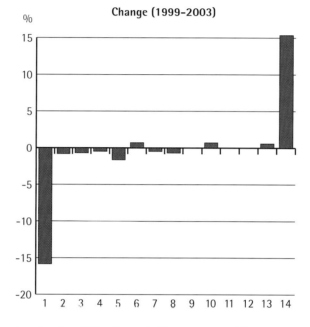

Notes: Category 1: tracts where less than 10% of households are asset wealthy; category 14: tracts where more than 40% of households are asset wealthy. See Figure 8, page 35, for full details of the 14 categories.

Poor health

Geographically referenced data on working-age claimants of IB similar to that on JSA claimants used in the section on 'Unemployment' (Chapter 8, page 72) were obtained from the WPLS, and used to estimate the geography of poor health across Britain. These data, along with the same denominator estimates used for the JSA analysis, were used to compare the proportion of each tract's working-age population claiming IB in 2000 and 2005. Map 34 shows the geographical distribution of IB claimants in 2000. This demonstrates a stark geographical divide between areas with high and low proportions of the working-age population claiming IB. The fifth of tracts with the lowest levels are almost all in south east and central England. The fifth of tracts with the highest levels are mostly in the valleys of south Wales, cities of the midlands and north of England and Scotland, especially in and around Glasgow.

The map of change in Map 35 is less clear. Increases of 20% or more are found mostly around London, but also in parts of north Yorkshire and Aberdeenshire. The largest decreases in the proportion of working-age people claiming IB are widespread, through Wales, northern England and especially around Glasgow. Figures 22 and 23 replicate the JSA graphs, presented above, for IB. There may be an interdependence between IB and JSA with claimants switching between benefits, which may influence the geographical patterns presented here. Figures 22 and 23 demonstrate that while most tracts experienced a small increase in IB claimants, those tracts with the very lowest claimant rates and the very highest breadline poverty rates in 2000 experienced small falls in IB claimant

Map 34: Geographical distribution of IB claimants (August 2000)

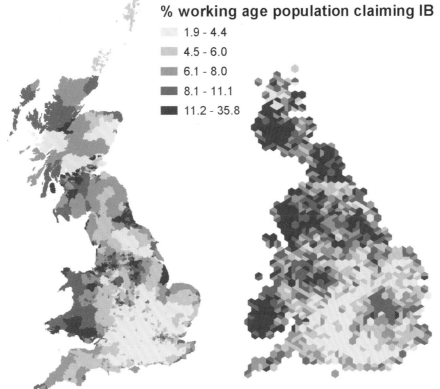

% working age population claiming IB

- 1.9 - 4.4
- 4.5 - 6.0
- 6.1 - 8.0
- 8.1 - 11.1
- 11.2 - 35.8

Tracts by quintile of working age IB claimant %, August 2000

Map 35: Geographical distribution of change in IB claimants (2000–05)

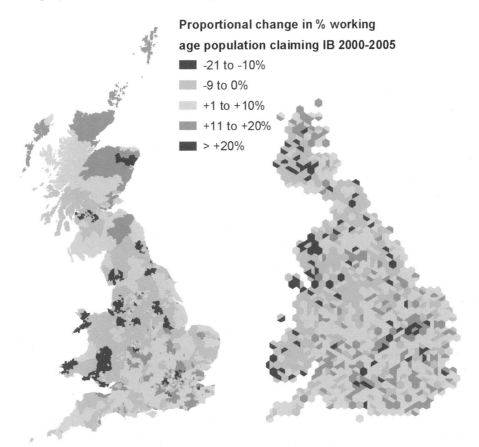

Proportional change in % working age population claiming IB 2000-2005

- -21 to -10%
- -9 to 0%
- +1 to +10%
- +11 to +20%
- > +20%

Figure 22: Absolute and proportional change in tract IB claimant percentages (2000–05), by IB claimant % decile

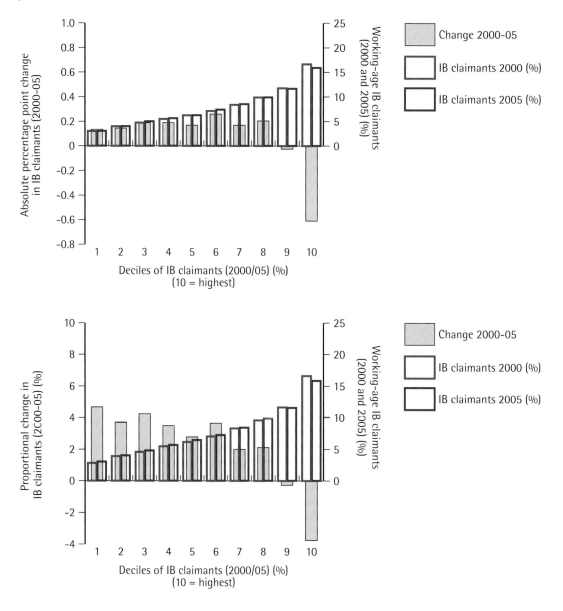

rates. Since claimant rates have gone up everywhere else, these graphs would seem to indicate the impact of efforts targeted at the very poorest and least healthy communities to reduce the numbers of people on IB. They may also reflect to some extent the diminishing numbers of people that are on IB through industrially related illness, due to deindustrialisation. These patterns are also in accordance with recent research (Alcock et al, 2003; Beatty and Fothergill, 2005; Fothergill and Smith, 2005; Fothergill and Wilson, 2006) who also suggested that there are very high numbers of people on IB in the older industrial areas of the North, Scotland and Wales, reflecting 'hidden unemployment' on a grand scale.

Finally, the spatial concentration analysis presented in Map 36 helps to clarify the geographical pattern of change. Clusters of increases in claimants are found through north eastern Scotland and the borders, some northern cities (especially Bradford and Sheffield), the periphery of London and parts of the West Country. The cluster of decreases appears predominantly in Wales and the North Midlands, into northern England and around Glasgow. Interestingly, there are quite a number of high spatial outliers (increases proximal to decreases) in the same areas.

Figure 23: Absolute and proportional change in tract IB claimant percentages (2000–05), by breadline poverty decile (2000)

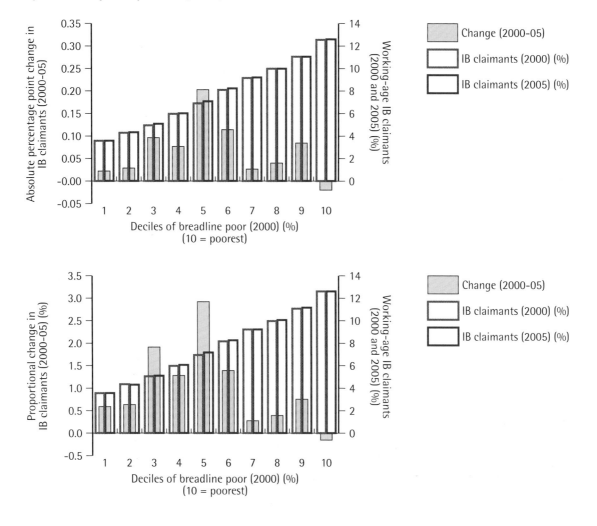

Map 36: Spatial concentration analysis of the change in % of the working-age population claiming IB (2000–05)

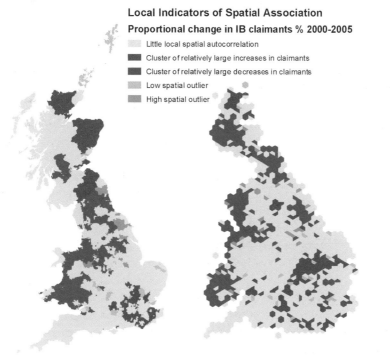

9

Discussion

National understanding of poverty and wealth tends to be largely aspatial. National debate tends to be concerned with the proportions of households that fall into each category at each point in time: how many households are poor or wealthy, just how poor are the poor, and what share of wealth do the wealthiest have? What this report attempts to show is that there is another set of questions that are also important. Where do the wealthy and the poor live? Are they becoming more geographically mixed or more estranged from each other spatially as well as socially? Furthermore, where is poverty and wealth most strongly concentrated and most evenly spread? Where are the fewest and greatest proportions of households neither poor nor rich? We know that the geography of poverty does not change particularly quickly (Dorling et al, 2000), but it is important to understand how it has and does change over time, and equally importantly how the geography of wealth develops.

Research on poverty in Britain typically concentrates on patterns of poverty and in doing so tends to implicitly define a general group of 'non-poor' to whom the poor are in effect always contrasted. However, those households that are not poor are not a uniform group. A fraction of the wealth of just a proportion of the richest would be enough, if transferred perfectly, to tip all those who were materially poor above any conventional poverty line. In this report we have attempted to present a fairer picture of how we are divided by poverty and wealth by distinguishing between the core poor (the poorest of the poor); the breadline poor (those excluded from the norms of society due to lack of material resources); those households who are neither rich, nor poor; the asset wealthy (those who, on the basis of their housing wealth, can expect to pay Inheritance Tax); and the exclusive wealthy (those able to exclude themselves from the norms of society by using their wealth).

It is important to stress that we are looking at social divides far more important than those reflected merely by income. Many of the most wealthy in society need not work and do not draw a conventional income, just as many of the poorest often cannot work and have little conventional income. Poverty and wealth are fundamentally about being excluded from society or included in it. It is not just the poor that are excluded, and, as we have shown above, in some places there is less and less of a 'normal' society for anyone to be included in. For too long we have studied poverty without considering wealth.

This report makes many findings that should appear obvious after first reading but which are too often not understood in national debate. For instance, the numbers of poor and rich households do not tend to rise together. Poverty tends to rise as the proportion of wealth held by the best-off increases – but that does not necessarily imply more wealthy households – just that wealthier households have become wealthier still. In short our report shows that as breadline poverty has increased, so too has the share of wealth held by the wealthiest, but the proportion of households that are asset wealthy has actually fallen. People may believe (and repeatedly be told) that on average they are better off but in distributional terms most has gone to those who already held most, and more can no longer partake in the norms of society due to breadline poverty.

At the extremes we do find a fall in the proportion of households who are core poor – households who are simultaneously income poor, necessities/deprivation poor and subjectively (know they are) poor – falling back by the year 2000 to the level last attained in 1980. Given the introduction of a Minimum Wage, Working Families and Pension Tax Credits and many other innovations in recent years, it would be surprising if this were not the case, but it is still good news to see this reversal in a trend confirmed. However, we also find that the proportion who are exclusive wealthy has remained relatively stable since 1970. Also, there were, for the first time, by the year 2000 large neighbourhoods in Britain where the majority of households were living below the breadline – not core poor – but not able to partake in the norms of society as defined at that time. There are, however, many fewer areas where over a fifth of households are core poor in the year 2000 as compared with 1990 or 1970.

When changes over time are considered, a key finding is that there is little change in the relative ranks of areas over time and changes tend to be linear. That is, when poverty rises it tends to rise everywhere, but slightly more where it was most common to begin with (and vice versa when it falls). Wealth shows less clear-cut trends, partly because of the way we have to estimate it here, but again areas that were wealthy in the past tend to remain so, if not become wealthier still. Most interesting and certainly unexpected when this work began is the geography to those households who are neither rich nor poor. Over time it has become clear that there is less and less room in the south for them; they have either moved elsewhere, or become wealthy or poor.

Various arguments are made as to the mechanisms that underly increases in inequality; two key ones are that it is caused to some extent by demographic change or by differential migration. The interpretation of these causal mechanisms, if in fact true, could perhaps be that changes in the degree of inequality are in part due to population changes and movements, which are difficult to change using social policies. A recent report from the IPPR has suggested that, '... it is likely that a substantial proportion of the rise in inequality between 1979 and 2003/04 was due to demographic change' (Dixon and Margo, 2006, p 3). However, this statement is perhaps not borne out by the evidence presented in that same report. In Table A2.1 (Dixon and Margo, 2006, p 159), Dixon and Margo analyse income data from the Family Expenditure/Resources Surveys and report that without adjusting for demographic change, the income Gini coefficient changed from 0.25 in 1979 to 0.34 in 2003/04, a substantial increase in income inequality. However, after adjusting for demographic change over that period, they find the Gini coefficient for 2003/04 to be 0.322, a very small drop from the unadjusted figure of 0.34. This would seem to suggest, for this analysis at least, that demographic change has had very little to do with rising inequality over the 1980s and 1990s.

In terms of internal migration, it is possible that differential movement of the population results in increasing geographical inequality. For example, if well educated and highly skilled people are more likely to move towards places with good job (and hence income) opportunities than are people with fewer skills and lower educational attainment, this differential movement will result in poor places becoming poorer and wealthy places becoming wealthier (Gibbons et al, 2005). There is now ample evidence that university graduates and other groups who tend to be well remunerated have become ever more concentrated in parts of London and the south east of England despite also growing in number (Dorling, 2005). This internal migration will have inevitably displaced other groups who could no longer move in, in similar numbers to the past, to the areas now seeing increasing concentrations of the relatively young and affluent.

In the section on 'Polarisation' (Chapter 6, page 28), we showed that the very poorest areas in 1970 lost substantial numbers of people over the following 30 years, although most of the loss was in the 1970s. Similarly, the wealthiest areas in 1980 gained population over the following 20 years. What these findings mean for the study depends on who it is that has been leaving areas of decline and who has been moving into now more densely populated wealthy areas. Although a detailed analysis of the 1% Office for National Statistics (ONS) Longitudinal Study might help answer this question, and would be warranted, it does not take a huge leap of imagination to infer that those that were most able were more likely to have left poorer areas, and those best resourced helped boost the population of the most affluent places (Boyle et al, 2004; Norman et al, 2005). Increasing access to cars over the past three decades has allowed the population who can to segregate further.

Our report ends by looking beyond 2000 for clues as to the direction in which trends in inequality and polarisation may now be moving. These analyses show mixed trends. We see encouraging signs of greater reductions in JSA claimants between 2000 and 2005 in areas with higher claimant and poverty rates. However, analysis of income data indicated increasing polarisation, with those areas with the highest average incomes in 2003 experiencing the greatest increases to 2005, and those with the lowest incomes experiencing substantial declines. The relationship between JSA claimant rates and actual worklessness is not necessarily straightforward, but, this aside, the contradictory findings between the JSA and income analyses may indicate that lack of paid employment is becoming a less useful indicator of poverty.

IB claimant rates during 2000-05 increased across most areas, but fell in those tracts falling into the very highest claimant and poverty rate deciles. This might reflect the effects of policies targeted specifically at these areas, such as Pathways to Work (although these effects are likely to be limited, as it has been suggested elsewhere that they may not be anywhere near reaching their targets; see Fothergill and Wilson, 2006). In absolute terms, young people's HE participation increased to a similar extent in the areas with the highest and lowest rates, comparing the cohort due to graduate around 1997-2001 and that due to graduate around 2001-05. However, this translates to a trend of greater proportional increase among those tracts with lower participation rates, therefore a trend towards reduced geographical inequality. In terms of asset wealthy households, there was a strong trend for greater absolute increases between 1999 and 2003 in tracts with higher levels to begin with. Again, however, this trend in absolute terms is matched by the opposite trend of greater proportional increase in those tracts with the lowest levels of wealth to begin with.

10

Conclusions

In this report we have looked in some detail at measures of the polarisation of each of the five poverty/wealth groups over four or more time periods in 1,282 areas. Our findings can be summarised as seeing over the 30 years from 1970 increases in the populations of areas classified as having a very high rate of breadline poverty. Similarly, in 2000 we find increases in the population living in neighbourhoods where an extremely high proportion are wealthy, as compared to 1980.

To aid in the interpretation of all the data and figures produced we mapped where poverty and wealth have been most strongly spatially clustered at each point in time. Many of the patterns are quite simple, have changed only slowly and confirm just how divided Britain is as a nation of rich and poor, often living apart with no space for those in between where space is most contested (in the South East). We have provided a series of local studies to elaborate further.

The results of analysis of segregation (dissimilarity), along with those of polarisation and spatial concentration, support the conclusion that with respect to both poverty and wealth, Britain became increasingly segregated and polarised over the past two or three decades of the 20th century. Particularly notable is the clustering of poverty and low wealth in urban areas, and the concentration of wealth (especially with regard to exclusively wealthy households) in the South East of England.

The improvements noted since 2000, notably in JSA and IB claimants, and to a tangential extent in HE participation, should be applauded. However, the fact that they represent just the beginnings of tackling disparity is obvious when the magnitude of progress in the right direction is seen in the context of the existing degree of inequality. Further, we should note that in many cases inequality falls in relative terms once it can no longer rise. For instance when three quarters of children living in the best-off tracts in Britain go to university, the rate there cannot double; when only a few per cent participate in the poorest tracts, the rate can double with little absolute change. When simple inequalities in rates are this extensive, what begins to matter is which university young people attend, how likely they are to complete the course, and new inequalities may become apparent. This is a fruitful area for further research.

Those analyses regarding years since 2000 are subject to limitations in relation to geographical detail and length of time series. In order to understand better how patterns of poverty and wealth have developed in the years since 2000 and will develop into the future, in the context of what we know about previous decades, censuses of 2011 and beyond are crucial. Furthermore, if we are to gain greater insight into the geography of wealth and wealthy people, the development of questions in the census to discern those with sufficient wealth to 'opt out' of societal norms will be vital.

The fact that this report has taught its authors so much about the subject of the geography of wealth should help illustrate just how little we know about that side to the poverty–wealth divide to life and society in Britain today. A generation has grown up since Peter Townsend and Abel-Smith's survey of 1967/68 was first out 'into the field'. In Britain, over the course of the three decades that followed, slowly and not particularly steadily, more and more families became excluded from what it was normal to be able to do. That was not the direction of the trend at first; things were getting better in the 1970s. In the most recent period the very worst of what was achieved by 1990 has been reversed, but little more. There was also no great spreading of wealth, and those that had amassed most to begin with, now sit on more than ever before.

The last official inquiry into wealth reported in 1979 (Royal Commission on the Distribution of Income and Wealth, 1979). There has not been one since, although a new National Statistics Wealth and Assets Survey has been in the field since July 2006, and is likely to produce results by the end of 2007. Trends since 2000 are mixed; absolute increases in the prevalence of wealthy households have been greatest in the wealthiest areas, although the trend in proportional increases is the opposite. The trend for incomes is less encouraging, indicating substantial geographical income polarisation over the short period 2003-05.

Before we become pessimistic over the prospect for progressive change, however, we should remember that one key thing has changed for ever in British society since the end of the 1960s. In 1968, at the time of the first poverty survey, there were only 200,000 students allowed to attend university in Britain (Davies, 1994). By 2000/02 there were over two million (HESA, 2006). A ten-fold increase has occurred in a generation, and now a third of 18- and 19-year-olds go to university. This figure is over two fifths when it is measured as a proportion of those aged under 30, a proportion that is supposed to attain 50% by the year 2010. It remains to be seen how a young population, half of whom have gone to a university, will accept a place in the kind of society we have built for them over the course of the years 1968-2005.

Around the same time as Townsend's survey was in the field the philosopher John Rawls was theorising a game, which he published in 1971 (Rawls, 1971). In the game you get to choose the kind of society you would like to live in, but not your place in it. His example was hypothetical. It was a game that at the time only the tiny group of those allowed to learn then knew of. He described a world that was fairly equitable and one that was quite unequal and asked which you would choose. His design was fantasy. What we have described in this report is real. Who wants to be born in a neighbourhood where, odds on, you will grow up poor? Who wants to be born average where so many are poor, where the rich are gaining more and more and the exclusive rich are such a tiny group? Who will put up with that and who is going to change this?

References

Alcock, P., Beatty, C., Fothergill, S., Macmillan, R. and Yeandle, S. (2003) *Work to welfare: How men become detached from the labour market*, Cambridge: Cambridge University Press.

Anselin, L. (1995) 'Local Indicators of Spatial Association LISA', *Geographical Analysis*, vol 27, pp 93-115.

Beatty, C. and Fothergill, S. (2005) 'The diversion from "unemployment" to "sickness" across British regions and districts', *Regional Studies*, vol 39, pp 837-54.

Beveridge, W. (1942) *Social insurance and allied services*, Cmnd 6404, London: HMSO (reprinted in G. Davey Smith, D. Dorling and M. Shaw [eds] [2001] *Poverty, inequality and health in Britain: 1800-2000: A reader*, Bristol: The Policy Press).

Boyle, P., Norman, P. and Rees, P. (2004) 'Changing places: do changes in the relative deprivation of areas influence limiting long-term illness and mortality among non-migrant people living in non-deprived households?', *Social Science & Medicine*, vol 58, pp 2459-71.

Bradshaw, J.R. (1972a) 'The concept of social need', *New Society*, vol 496, pp 640-3.

Bradshaw, J.R. (1972b) 'The taxonomy of social need', in G. McLachlan (ed) *Problems and progress in medical care*, Oxford: Oxford University Press.

Bradshaw, J.R. (1994) 'The conceptualisation and measurement of need: a social policy perspective', in J. Popay and G. Williams (eds) *Researching the people's* health, London: Routledge.

Bradshaw, J.R. and Finch, N. (2003) 'Overlaps in dimensions of poverty', *Journal of Social Policy*, vol 32, pp 513-25.

Brewer, M., Goodman, A. and Leicester, A. (2006b) *Poverty in Britain: What can we learn from household spending?*, York: Joseph Rowntree Foundation (www.jrf.org.uk/bookshop/eBooks/9781861348555.pdf, 27/04/2006).

Brewer, M., Goodman, A., Shaw, J. and Sibieta, L. (2006a) *Poverty and inequality in Britain: 2006*, London: Institute for Fiscal Studies (www.ifs.org.uk/publications.php?publication_id=3575, 27/04/2006).

Corver, M. (2005) *Young participation in higher education*, HEFCE 2005/03, Bristol: Higher Education Funding Council for England.

Davies, G. (1994) *Overview of recent developments in HE*, Bristol: HEFCE (www.hefce.ac.uk/Pubs/hefce/1994/m2_94.htm, 17/7/2006)

Dixon, M. and Margo, J. (2006) *Population politics*, London: Institute for Public Policy Research.

Dorling, D. (2005) *A human geography of the UK*, London: Sage Publications.

Dorling, D. and Woodward, R. (1996) 'Social polarisation 1971-1991: a micro-geographical analysis of Britain', *Progress in Planning*, vol 45 (all pages).

Dorling, D., Gentle, C. and Cornford, J. (1994) 'Negative equity in 1990s Britain', *Urban Studies*, vol 31, no 2, pp 181-99.

Dorling, D., Mitchell, R., Shaw, M., Orford, S. and Davey Smith, G. (2000) 'The ghost of Christmas past: health effects of poverty in London in 1896 and 1991', *British Medical Journal*, vol 321, pp 1547-51.

DWP (Department for Work and Pensions) (2002) *Measuring child poverty: Consultation document*, London: DWP (www.dwp.gov.uk/ofa/related/measuring_child_poverty.pdf, 26/06/2006).

DWP (2003) *Measuring child poverty*, London: DWP (www.dwp.gov.uk/ofa/related/final_conclusions.pdf, 30/11/2006).

DWP (2005) *Work and Pensions Longitudinal Study – List of uses* (www.dwp.gov.uk/asd/longitudinal_study/WPLS_Uses.pdf, 4/12/2006).

Evans, M. and Scarborough, J. (2006) *Can current policy end child poverty in Britain by 2020?*, York: Joseph Rowntree Foundation.

Fotheringham, A.S., Brunsdon, C. and Charlton, M.E. (2002) *Geographically weighted regression: The analysis of spatially varying relationships*, Chichester: Wiley.

Fothergill, S. and Smith, J.G. (2005) *Mobilising Britain's missing workforce: Unemployment, incapacity benefit and the regions*, London: Catalyst Forum (www.catalystforum.org.uk).

Fothergill, S. and Wilson, I. (2006) *A million off incapacity benefit: How achievable is the government's target?*, Report commissioned by Scope, Sheffield Hallam University (www.shu.ac.uk/cresr/downloads/reports/A%20Million%20Off%20Incapacity%20Benefit.pdf, 27/11/2006).

Gibbons, S., Green, A., Gregg, P. and Machin, S. (2005) 'Is Britain pulling apart? Area inequalities in employment, education and crime', in N. Pearce and W. Paxton (eds) *Social justice: Building a fairer Britain*, London: Institute for Public Policy Research.

Gordon, D. and Pantazis, C. (eds) (1997) *Breadline Britain in the 1990s*, Aldershot: Ashgate.

Gordon, D., Adelman, A., Ashworth, K., Bradshaw, J.R., Levitas, R., Middleton, S., Pantazis, C., Patsios, D., Payne, S., Townsend, P. and Williams, J. (2000) *Poverty and social exclusion in Britain*, York: Joseph Rowntree Foundation.

Gregory, I., Southall, H. and Dorling, D. (2000) 'A century of poverty in England and Wales, 1898-1998: a geographical analysis', in J.R. Bradshaw and R. Sainsbury (eds) *Researching poverty*, Aldershot: Ashgate.

HESA (Higher Education Statistics Agency) (2006) *Higher Education Statistics for the United Kingdom 2004/5* (www.hesa.ac.uk/press/pr105/pr105.htm, 25/11/2006).

Hirsch, D. (2006) *What will it take to end child poverty? Firing on all cylinders*, York: Joseph Rowntree Foundation.

IPPR (Institute for Public Policy Research) (2004) *Fairer inheritance tax needed to respond to rising wealth inequality* (www.ippr.org.uk/pressreleases/archive.asp?id=812, 27/04/2006).

Jargowsky, P. (2003) *Stunning progress, hidden problems: The dramatic decline of concentrated poverty in the 1990s*, Washington, DC: The Brookings Institution.

Lansley, S. (2006) *Rich Britain: The rise and rise of the new super-wealthy*, London: Politico's Publishing Ltd.

Leyshon, A., Signoretta, P., Knights, D., Alferoff, C. and Burton, D. (2006) 'Walking with moneylenders: the ecology of the UK home collected credit industry', *Urban Studies*, vol 43, no 1, pp 161-86.

Lupton, R. (2003) *Poverty street: The dynamics of neighbourhood decline and renewal*, Bristol: The Policy Press.

Lupton, R. (2005) *Changing neighbourhoods? Mapping the geography of poverty and worklessness using the 1991 and 2001 Census*, CASE-Brookings Census Brief 3 (http://sticerd.lse.ac.uk/dps/case/CBCB/census3.pdf, 24/7/2006).

Mack, J. and Lansley, S. (1985) *Poor Britain*, London: George Allen & Unwin.

Medeiros, M. (2006) *Poverty, inequality and redistribution: A methodology to define the rich*, UNDP Working Paper 18 (www.undp-povertycentre.org/ipcpublications.htm, 22/05/2006).

National Statistics (2006a) *Share of the wealth: 1% of population owns 21% of wealth* (www.statistics.gov.uk/cci/nugget.asp?id=2, 17/05/2006).

National Statistics (2006b) *The effects of taxes and benefits on household income, 2004-05* (www.statistics.gov.uk/cci/article.asp?id=1551, 17/05/2006).

National Statistics (2006c) *Social trends, no 36*, London: The Stationery Office.

Norman, P., Boyle, P. and Rees, P. (2005) 'Selective migration, health and deprivation: a longitudinal analysis', *Social Science & Medicine*, vol 60, no 12, pp 2755-71.

Orford, S. (2004) 'Identifying and comparing changes in the spatial concentrations of urban poverty and affluence: a case study of inner London', *Computers Environment and Urban Systems*, vol 28, pp 701-17.

Palmer, G., Kenway, P. and Wilcox, S. (2006) *Housing and neighbourhoods monitor*, London: New Policy Institute.

Pantazis, C., Gordon, D. and Levitas, R. (eds) (2006) *Poverty and social exclusion in Britain*, Bristol: The Policy Press.

Paxton, W. and Dixon, M. (2004) *The state of the nation: An audit of social justice*, London: Institute for Public Policy Research (www.ippr.org.uk/ecomm/files/stateofnation.pdf, 27/04/2006).

Philo, C. (ed) (1995) *Off the map: The social geography of poverty in the UK*, London: Child Poverty Action Group, pp 103-22.

Rawls, J. (1971) *A theory of justice*, Oxford: Oxford University Press.

Rentoul, J. (1987) *The rich get richer: The growth of inequality in Britain in the 1980s*, London: HarperCollins.

Rio Expert Group on Poverty Statistics (2006) *Compendium of best practices in poverty measurement*, Rio de Janeiro, September (www.ibge.gov.br/poverty/pdf/rio_group_compendium.pdf, 30/11/2006).

Royal Commission on the Distribution of Income and Wealth (1979) *Royal Commission on the distribution of income and wealth, Report no 8*, London: HMSO.

Rowntree, B.S. (1901, reissued 2000) *Poverty: A study of town life* (centenary edn), Bristol: The Policy Press.

SASI (Social and Spatial Inequalities) Research Group (2006) 'Tracts information', SASI Research Group, University of Sheffield (www.sasi.group.shef.ac.uk/tracts/index.htm, 16/05/2006).

Schifferes, S. (1986) *The rich in Britain, New Society*, 22 August.

Scott, J. (1994) *Poverty and wealth: Citizenship, deprivation and privilege*, London, Longman.

Sutherland, H., Sefton, T. and Piachaud, D. (2003) *Progress on poverty, 1997 to 2003/4*, York: Joseph Rowntree Foundation (www.jrf.org.uk/knowledge/findings/socialpolicy/043.asp, 27/04/2006).

Thomas, B. and Dorling, D. (2004) *Investigation report: Know your place*, London: Shelter (http://england.shelter.org.uk/policy/policy-825.cfm/plitem/160, 27/04/2006).

Tobler, W.R. (1970) 'A computer movie simulating urban growth in the Detroit region', *Economic Geography*, vol 46 (Suppl), pp 234-40.

Townsend, P. (1979) *Poverty in the United Kingdom: A survey of household resources and standards of living*, London: Penguin Books and Allen Lane.

Toynbee, P. (2006) 'Downsizing dreams', *The Guardian*, 8 April (http://books.guardian.co.uk/review/story/0,,1749089,00.html, 23/08/2006).

Tulip (2002) *Britain's millionaires: The powerhouse of private investment*, London: Tulip Financial Research.

Tunstall, R. and Coulter, A. (2006) *Twenty-five years on twenty estates: Turning the tide?*, Bristol/York: The Policy Press/Joseph Rowntree Foundation (free electronic copies can be downloaded from www.jrf.org.uk).

Veblen, T. (1899, 1994 edn) *The theory of the leisure class*, London: Penguin Books.

Vickers, D. (2005) *The national classification of census output areas* (http://sasi.group.shef.ac.uk/area_classification/index.html, 10/11/2006).

Whelan, C.T., Layte, R., Maitre, B. and Nolan, B. (2001) 'Income, deprivation and economic strain: an analysis of the European Community Household Panel', *European Sociological Review*, vol 17, no 4, pp 357-72.

Winnett, R. (2006) 'Stone me ... Tony Hancock's suburb is UK's healthiest', *The Sunday Times*, 12 February, p 14.

Wolff, E.N. (1998) 'Recent trends in the size distribution of household wealth', *Journal of Economic Perspectives*, vol 12, pp 131-50.

Appendix 1: Methods

Breadline and core poverty

There have been only four nationally representative scientific surveys of poverty in the past 50 years, listed below. All were funded by the Joseph Rowntree Foundation and two received additional funding from London Weekend Television. All were undertaken by academics, and all were relatively small:

- *Poverty in the United Kingdom: A survey of household resources and standards of living*, 1967-69, 2,052 households (Townsend, 1979).
- *Living in Britain*, 1983, 1,174 households, published as *Poor Britain* (Mack and Lansley, 1985).
- *Breadline Britain*, 1990, 1,831 households (Gordon and Pantazis, 1997).
- *Poverty and Social Exclusion Survey*, 1999, 1,534 households (Gordon et al, 2000).

Despite the restricted sample sizes, the above surveys reflect a broadly comparable relative approach to the definition and measurement of poverty. By adopting a synthetic modelling approach, it is therefore technically possible to examine the spatial distribution of area poverty over time based on four discrete time slices: 1967-69 (1971 Census); 1983 (1981 Census); 1990 (1991 Census); and 1999 (2001 Census) using a comparable methodology.

This approach involves the construction of reliable, valid and additive deprivation indices for each of the four surveys, and subsequently developing summary, binary indicators of 'breadline poverty' based on the 'fit' between material and social deprivation on the one hand, and net equivilised household income on the other. It is also possible to measure the extent of 'core poverty' based on the overlap between low income, material and social deprivation and subjective poverty (described in the section on 'Poverty' in Chapter 3, page 10). Using a logistic regression modelling approach the social and demographic predictors of poverty can then be estimated and the derived weightings applied to census small area statistics (for a detailed discussion of the logistic regression model that we used see Working Paper 1, http://sasi.group.shef.ac.uk/research/transformation).

These census weightings for both breadline and core poverty measures at each time period are given in Table A1 below. The total number of poor households is obtained by summing the households from census data (for any geographical unit, such as ward or local authority area) using the weightings given. For example, the number of core poor households in 1970 is:

7% of households lacking bath/shower +
14% of households lacking a car +
11% of households renting from private landlord +
11% of households where head of household is a manual worker +
15% of single-pensioner households +
7% of pensioner couple households

This total would be divided by the total number of households to give the proportion of core poor households.

Table A1: Census weightings used to calculate breadline and core poor measures for each time period

Time period and data sources	Census variable	Bread-line poor (%)	Core poor (%)
1970 1968 Poverty Survey 1971 Census	Households lacking bath/shower	17	7
	Households lacking a car	25	14
	Households renting from local authority	8	
	Households renting from private landlord	14	11
	Head of household is manual worker	6	11
	Overcrowded households	9	
	Single-pensioner households	14	15
	Pensioner couple households	6	7
1980 1983 Poverty Survey 1981 Census	Households lacking exclusive use of bath or indoor toilet	34	13
	Households sharing accommodation	28	
	Households lacking access to a car	14	8
	Households living in council accommodation	17	9
	Households living in private rental or 'other' accommodation	12	
	Unemployed households	18	17
	Households containing three or more dependent children	15	11
	Lone-parent households		11
1990 1990 Poverty Survey 1991 Census	Lone-parent households	22	20
	Head of household is unskilled worker	17	16
	Household tenure not owned outright or buying with mortgage	19	9
	Households lacking a car	26	17
	Households with three or more dependent children	13	10
	Unemployed households	16	16
	Single-pensioner households	9	6
2000 1999 Poverty Survey 2001 Census	Overcrowded households (more than one person per room)	58	22
	Households renting from local authority or housing association	36	16
	Lone-parent households	32	17
	Households with an unemployed household reference person (HRP)	30	12
	Households with no car	18	5
	Households renting from a private landlord	17	7
	Households with a member with a limiting long-term illness	16	10
	Households with no central heating or not having sole use of amenities	14	5
	Households with HRP in NS-SEC 6, 7 or 8	11	

The breadline poverty measure (Breadline Britain Index) had been calculated previously for 1990 and 1999, and methods and results are described in the reports referenced above. This study developed novel methods to estimate the prevalence of core poverty, and produced both measures for tract geography for each of the four time periods, including slightly revised versions of the original breadline poverty measures for 1990 and 1999. A detailed discussion of the methods used to calculate breadline and core poverty using the 1983 Survey and the 1981 Census, and full details of the census variables and weightings are included in the Working Paper referred to above and available at www.sasi.group.shef.ac.uk/research/transformation

Asset wealthy method

The section on 'Wealth' (Chapter 3, page 12) briefly describes the methodology developed to calculate the asset wealthy measures. Further details of the method are given here.

The data used were developed for a previous project, reported in Thomas and Dorling (2004). They consisted of, for each property type (detached, semi-detached, terrace or flat) in each tract, a count of the number of houses/flats owned outright, the number being bought with a mortgage, and the average price of that type of property in the tract. Data were also available for households renting their home, but these households do not own any housing equity, so none of them are considered wealthy by this measure.

These data were used to estimate the number of households with housing equity (wealth) over a set threshold, as described in the section on 'Wealth') (Chapter 3, page 12). This analysis was carried out in the following stages:

1. Households owning their home outright are assumed to have housing equity equivalent to the average price of that type of property in that tract.

2. The housing equity owned by those people buying their home with a mortgage is lower than the equity owned by those who own outright, and is estimated using the adjustment to tract average property price used in Thomas and Dorling (2004). This is based on the assumption that the more households in an area that own outright, the closer those with a mortgage are to paying off the mortgage. The average equity held by a household buying their property with a mortgage is therefore set equal to the average house price in that area, multiplied by the proportion of home owners that own outright. That is, if p_d is the average price of a detached house in a tract, o_d is the number of detached houses owned outright, and b_d is the number of detached houses being bought with a mortgage, the average equity held by households in detached houses with mortgages is:

$$p_d \times (o_d/(o_d + b_d))$$

3. Estimate a sorted distribution of housing equity across house types for each tract:
   - Construct ordered average prices for each tract.
   - Generate variables p_1, p_2, p_3, p_4 (lowest to highest average price in tract); o_1-o_4 (number of properties of respective type owned outright)
     – For most tracts, flat price < terraced price < semi-detached price < detached price, so p_1 = average flat price, o_1 = number of flats owned outright, p_2 = average terraced price etc. The following assumes this ordering to be the case (prices and associated numbers of properties are simply re-ordered where not the case).
   - Similarly generate e_1-e_4 (average estimated equity for those buying with a mortgage) and b_1-b_4 (number of properties of respective type being bought with a mortgage).

4. Estimate maximum and minimum equity value for each property type for both owned and properties being bought with a mortgage:
   - Estimated maximum flat equity (owned) = mid-way between the average price of a flat and the average price of a terrace = p_{1max} = $(p_1 + p_2)/2$
   - Estimated minimum terrace equity (owned) = mid-way between the average price of a flat and the average price of a terrace = p_{2min} = $(p_1 + p_2)/2$
   - Estimated maximum terrace equity (owned) = mid-way between the average price of a terrace and the average price of a semi-detached = p_{2max} = $(p_2 + p_3)/2$
   - And so on, up to estimated maximum detached equity (owned) = detached price squared divided by semi-detached price = p_{4max} = $(p_4 \times p_4)/p_3$

- Estimated maximum flat equity (being bought) = mid-way between the average equity estimate of a flat being bought and the average equity estimate of a terrace = e_{1max} = $(e_1 + e_2)/2$
- And so on as for p_1-p_4.

We now have the following data/estimates for each tract:

Property type[a]	Number of properties	Minimum equity value	Maximum equity value
Flat, owned outright	o_1	n/a	p_{1max}
Terrace, owned outright	o_2	p_{2min}	p_{2max}
Semi-detached, owned outright	o_3	p_{3min}	p_{3max}
Detached, owned outright	o_4	p_{4min}	p_{4max}
Flat, being bought with mortgage	b_1	n/a	e_{1max}
Terrace, being bought with mortgage	b_2	e_{2min}	e_{2max}
Semi-detached, being bought with mortgage	b_3	e_{3min}	e_{3max}
Detached, being bought with mortgage	b_4	e_{4min}	e_{4max}

Note: [a] Assumes equity hierarchy: flat < terraced < semi-detached < detached; where this is not the case, the types are re-ordered, for example, if average flat equity is greater than terraced, o_1 is terraced and o_2 is flats; p_1 is terraced equity and p_2 is flat equity and so on.

5. Set the housing wealth threshold above which a household is classified as 'asset wealthy'. This is described in the section on 'Wealth' (Chapter 3, page 12), and is found by multiplying the contemporary Inheritance Tax threshold by the contemporary percentage of national wealth held as housing.

6. For each tract estimate the number of households of each type with housing wealth above the threshold (T) set in stage 5:
   - Owned:
     - If $T > p_{1max}$ then no household owning flats are assumed to be wealthy
     - If $T < p_{1max}$ the number of owned wealthy flat occupying households =

$$((p_{1max} - T)/p_{1max}) \times o_1$$

   ie in a tract with 100 owned flats where the maximum equity value of an owned flat is £100,000, if the threshold is £50,000, then 50 owned flat households are assumed to be wealthy.
   - If $T < p_{2min}$ all of the owned terraced houses (o_2) are assumed to contain wealthy households
   - If threshold $> p_{2min}$ but $< p_{2max}$ the number of wealthy terraced households =

$$((p_{2max} - T)/(p_{2max} - p_{2min})) \times o_2$$

   ie in a tract with 100 owned terraced houses where the minimum terrace is worth £100,000; the maximum terrace is worth £200,000 and if the threshold is £125,000, 75 owned terraced houses are assumed to be home to wealthy households.
   - Similar equations using p_3 and p_4 are used to estimate the numbers of wealthy semi-detached and detached owning households.
   - For households in property being bought with mortgages:
     - The same series of equations, substituting e_1 for p_1 (estimated equity rather than price) and b_1 for o_1 (number being bought rather than owned outright) are used to estimate the number of households of each property type that are asset wealthy.

- The number of asset wealthy flats, terraced, semi-detached and detached houses are then summed for both those being bought and owned outright to give the total number of asset wealthy households in the tract.

Exclusive wealthy method

A method was developed to use the Family Expenditure Surveys to generate an overall estimate of the proportion of households that are exclusive wealthy, defined below. For the main analysis series presented in the report, this national exclusive wealthy proportion is used to calibrate the asset wealthy methodology described above in order to produce exclusive wealth estimates for tracts at each time period. The alternative method mentioned in the report combined data from the surveys with geographically detailed census data in a similar way to the breadline methodology to produce weightings of census variables that might indicate 'wealth'. This alternative methodology was not used for the analysis for reasons discussed below.

Method overview

As with poverty, a 'wealth line' can also be defined theoretically, for example, by building on the work of UK sociologist John Scott (1994) and US radical economist Thorstein Veblen (1899). For Scott, individuals and households are 'wealthy' if their resource level is such that they would be able to voluntarily exclude themselves from participation in the normal activities of societies if they so chose. Similarly, Veblen's theory of the 'leisure class' defines a wealth line in which gradations of social status reflect consumption patterns and in particular the emergence of 'conspicuous consumption' as a social signifier of status.

However, although these and other approaches to the definition and measurement of wealth have been proposed (see also Rentoul, 1987; Wolff, 1998), to our knowledge no one has tried to operationalise the wealth line.

As with the analysis of poverty over time described elsewhere in this report, the overall goal of this approach seeks to derive a series of synthetic estimates of wealth based on regression modelling that can be applied to small area census statistics for the 1971-2001 period in Britain. However, the Family Expenditure Survey wealth models described here and elsewhere are based not only on different data sources and indicators but also a very different approach to determining a wealth threshold (based on cluster analysis). The research process involves four distinct phases:

1. Selection of data sources
2. Selection of wealth indicators
3. Deriving a wealth threshold
4. Modelling of Family Expenditure Survey wealth distributions.

Selection of data sources: the source of wealth data used here is the Family Expenditure Survey series, a large-scale annual survey of household expenditure based on household diaries. The survey is undertaken across the UK and is organised by government statisticians. Family Expenditure Survey household-level records have been matched on key wealth-based and demographic variables and samples have been pooled across waves so that the resultant models are based on datasets containing between 12,600 and 21,100 cases, as illustrated in Table A2. The potential for combining data from different years was limited by changes in the way data were collected and recorded.

Table A2: Family Expenditure Survey wealth model sample sizes (1970–2000)

Census year	Family Expenditure Survey year	Un–weighted *N*
1971	1970	6,228
	1971	7,087
	1972	6,867
	1970–72	**20,182**
1981	1980	6,810
	1981	7,394
	1980–81	**14,204**
1991	1990	6,907
	1991	6,919
	1992	7,279
	1990–92	**21,105**
2001	1999	6,510
	2000	6,115
	1999–2000	**12,625**

For each of the resulting period files (1970-72; 1980-81; 1990-92; 1999-2000) the sample data have been re-weighted to British census estimates based on the following variables harmonised with census definitions for the relevant period:

- *Household type:* single person; single pensioner; couple/couple with children; lone parent; other.
- *Housing tenure:* owner-occupier; local authority or housing authority rental; private rental; other.

Selection of wealth indicators: the selection of wealth indicators seeks to reflect the theoretical construction of wealth described above based on notions of self-exclusion (Scott, 1994) and conspicuous consumption (Veblen, 1899). In principle, different indicators of wealth could be used to operationalise these concepts at different time points. However, in practice relatively few Family Expenditure Survey variables directly tap these theoretical constructs and for consistency of approach we have used the following variables in each of the four Family Expenditure Survey wealth models:

Indicator	Description	Unit	Construct
nrooms	Rooms in household	N	Consumption
ncars	Cars owned by household	N	Consumption
newcar	Expenditure on a new car	£	Consumption
airtrvl	Expenditure on (overseas) air-travel	£	Exclusion
privhlth	Expenditure on private healthcare	£	Exclusion
hlthins	Expenditure on private health insurance	£	Exclusion
prived	Expenditure on private school fees	£	Exclusion
domserv	Expenditure on private domestic services	£	Exclusion
scndhse	Expenditure on a second home	£	Exclusion

Expenditure data for each period have been adjusted to prices in the census year to reflect changes in the Retail Price Index (RPI) within the period covered by the analysis (for example, 1970-72 prices adjusted to 1971).

Deriving a wealth threshold: based on the above set of observed variables it is possible to derive a wealth threshold defining wealthy and non-wealthy households using cluster analysis. Cluster analysis methods seek to reveal the underlying structure in a set of observed variables based on Euclidean geometry. This procedure attempts to identify relatively homogeneous groups of cases (or variables) based on selected characteristics – in this case household expenditure habits. The procedure is iterative, being based on an algorithm that starts with each case in a separate cluster and combines clusters based on statistical criteria.

The selected agglomeration method used in this study is Ward's method used to define a set of clusters of cases based on the observed values of the above variables. These clusters can then be simplified using K-means clustering to identify clusters of cases defined with respect to their consumption habits. Cluster analyses were performed using Clustan Graphics.

The results shown in the box below show group membership for each of the 20,182 cases included in the cluster model. The K-means clustering has identified five distinct groups ranging in size from 16 to 13,184 cases. The mean values for each cluster are shown for each of the variables used to derive cluster membership – in this case showing that the mean number of cars owned by households was less than one in Clusters 1 (0.688) and 3 (0.357). These clusters identifying 13,184 and 6,441 cases respectively – or 97.3% of cases – are 'average' and 'poor' households.

In contrast, Clusters 2, 4 and 5 define different fractions of the rich group comprising 557 cases (2.7%). It is interesting to note that households belonging to Cluster 4 have a very high expenditure on overseas air travel (£39.67) when compared to the other cluster. Likewise, households belonging to Cluster 5 have very high expenditure on new cars.

The relative distance of all clusters in multidimensional space from the sample mean is shown in the dendrogram opposite. A dendogram is a visual representation of the steps in a clustering solution that shows the clusters being combined and the values of the distance coefficients at each step. Again we can clearly see the difference between the average and poor groups on the one hand, and the rich groups on the other, which may be combined.

Here, income and expenditure data are equivilised using the Poverty and Social Exclusion Survey equivilisation method and adjusted to census year prices. Based on cluster membership it is therefore possible to define income and expenditure thresholds using standard statistical methods to identify 'exclusive wealthy' households:

- Respondents are defined as *exclusive wealthy* if their Poverty and Social Exclusion Survey equivilised household incomes *and* expenditures are *greater than the median of the rich group*[12] identified in the K-means cluster solution.
- Respondents are defined as *non-exclusive wealthy* if their Poverty and Social Exclusion Survey equivilised household incomes *and* expenditures are *less than the median of the rich group* identified in the K-means cluster solution.

---

[12] The 'rich group' comprises all households that belong to Clusters 2, 4 and 5.

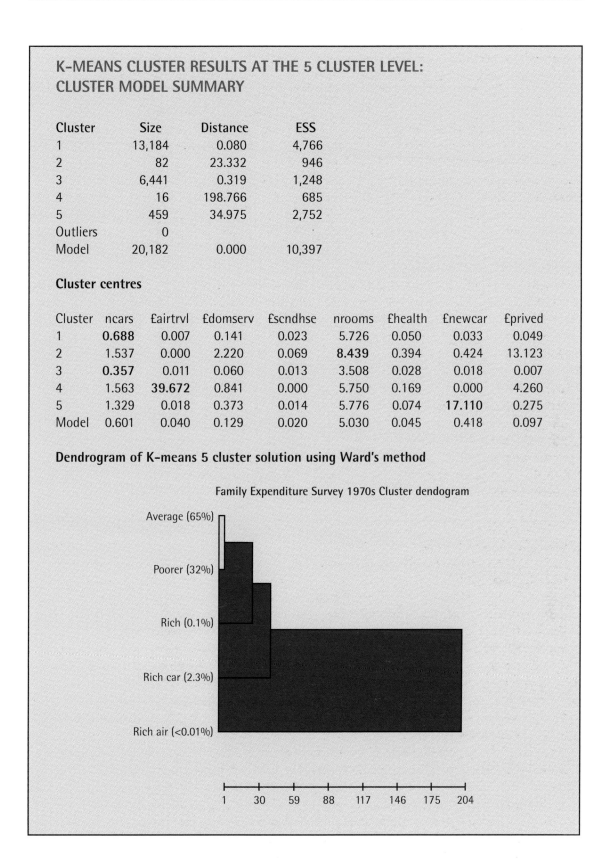

K-MEANS CLUSTER RESULTS AT THE 5 CLUSTER LEVEL: CLUSTER MODEL SUMMARY

Cluster	Size	Distance	ESS
1	13,184	0.080	4,766
2	82	23.332	946
3	6,441	0.319	1,248
4	16	198.766	685
5	459	34.975	2,752
Outliers	0		
Model	20,182	0.000	10,397

Cluster centres

Cluster	ncars	£airtrvl	£domserv	£scndhse	nrooms	£health	£newcar	£prived
1	**0.688**	0.007	0.141	0.023	5.726	0.050	0.033	0.049
2	1.537	0.000	2.220	0.069	**8.439**	0.394	0.424	13.123
3	**0.357**	0.011	0.060	0.013	3.508	0.028	0.018	0.007
4	1.563	**39.672**	0.841	0.000	5.750	0.169	0.000	4.260
5	1.329	0.018	0.373	0.014	5.776	0.074	**17.110**	0.275
Model	0.601	0.040	0.129	0.020	5.030	0.045	0.418	0.097

Dendrogram of K-means 5 cluster solution using Ward's method

Family Expenditure Survey 1970s Cluster dendogram

Average (65%)
Poorer (32%)
Rich (0.1%)
Rich car (2.3%)
Rich air (<0.01%)

1   30   59   88   117   146   175   204

Table A3 shows the relevant income and expenditure thresholds for each of the four pooled samples in raw pounds per week, adjusted for inflation, and expressed as a percentage of Family Expenditure Survey sample equivilised mean income and expenditure based on different definitions of the wealth thresholds (mean, median, 5% trimmed mean). Based on the median method the wealth threshold has risen, primarily between 1981 and 1991 and especially with respect to expenditure, relative to mean sample income and expenditure. As a result, the proportion of respondents identified as rich based on the median method falls from 6.9% in 1981 to 3.5% in 1991.

Table A3: Income and expenditure thresholds (£) and frequencies (%) for Family Expenditure Survey exclusive wealth (1971-2001)

	1971		1981		1991		2001	
	£	Ratio	£	Ratio	£	Ratio	£	Ratio
Weekly income thresholds (£)								
Mean	49.36	1.64	239.11	1.72	594.19	2.00	861.20	2.02
5% trimmed mean	45.73	1.52	213.11	1.53	500.72	1.68	744.11	1.75
Median	43.11	1.43	198.53	1.42	449.10	1.51	638.45	1.50
Weekly expenditure thresholds (£)								
Mean	44.36	1.83	201.63	1.94	589.02	2.73	719.48	2.21
5% trimmed mean	41.70	1.72	185.17	1.78	547.83	2.54	676.57	2.08
Median	39.18	1.62	169.27	1.63	489.26	2.27	629.86	1.94
Sample means (£)								
Poverty and Social Exclusion Survey income	30.16		139.38		297.36		426.40	
Poverty and Social Exclusion Survey expenditure	24.22		104.02		215.40		325.24	
Exclusive wealthy (%)								
Mean	4.5		3.2		1.5		2.8	
5% trimmed mean	5.9		4.9		2.4		4.0	
Median	7.4		6.9		3.5		5.6	

The overall proportions of exclusive wealthy households produced here were used to calibrate the asset wealthy methodology to produce exclusive wealth estimates for tracts at each time period, as described in the section on 'Wealth' (Chapter 3, page 12) of the report. The proportions derived using the 'median' method were used, since these larger figures would give more robust small area estimates for the geographical analyses. The following describes the alternative method, combining the Family Expenditure Survey analysis with the census to estimate exclusive wealth for tracts. As previously stated this alternative method was not eventually used for the analysis, for reasons described below.

Modelling of Family Expenditure Survey wealth: having identified Family Expenditure Survey wealth thresholds based on cluster analysis and applied these thresholds to the sample, it is possible to estimate the odds of wealth using logistic regression techniques and then to calibrate the resultant weights to the census. The predictor variables in each of the four Family Expenditure Survey models of wealth are common to both the Survey and the relevant census and have been harmonised with contemporary census definitions.

Results for all four models are shown in Table A4. The first output column shows the percentage of respondents within each category who are exclusive wealthy. The second output column shows the odds of wealth for each category in comparison with the relevant group outside the category (for example, not high social class, not owner-occupier, etc). The third output column shows the relative odds of being rich based on logistic regression and simultaneously taking into account the effect of the other predictors included in the model. Finally, the fourth output column shows the census weights to be applied to census small area statistics based on the (recalibrated) logistic regression coefficients (B).

Table A4: Family Expenditure Survey exclusive wealthy: univariate and multivariate analyses and census weights

	% Family Expenditure Survey rich	Univariate odds	Multivariate odds	Census weight
1971				
High social class (HRP)	21.7	6.53	4.551	0.0314
Owner-occupier	11.1	3.00	2.015	0.0145
No dependent children	9.9	3.79	8.174	0.0435
Respondent in work	9.3	2.61	2.958	0.0224
7+ rooms in household	18.2	3.25	2.127	0.0156
2+ cars in household	28.6	6.62	3.984	0.0286
ALL/Model R²	7.4		0.284	
1981				
High social class (HRP)	17.9	5.89	2.519	0.0314
Owner-occupier	10.5	6.24	2.518	0.0145
No dependent children	9.0	3.93	7.079	0.0435
Respondent in work	9.7	3.10	4.491	0.0224
7+ rooms in household	16.9	3.44	2.132	0.0156
2+ cars in household	17.5	4.47	2.351	0.0286
ALL/Model R²	6.9		0.270	
1991				
High social class (HRP)	10.4	7.24	3.766	0.0123
Respondent in work	5.5	4.74	1.948	0.0062
Owner-occupier	4.8	7.01	3.110	0.0105
No dependent children	4.2	2.25	4.715	0.0144
7+ rooms in household	10.4	4.94	2.549	0.0087
2+ cars in household	8.2	4.48	2.051	0.0067
ALL/Model R²	3.5		0.222	
2001				
High social class (HRP)	14.5	8.08	4.219	0.0226
Respondent in work	8.7	7.70	3.695	0.0206
Owner-occupier	7.4	4.57	1.968	0.0106
No dependent children	6.6	1.92	4.214	0.0226
7+ rooms in household	12.0	3.47	2.117	0.0118
2+ cars in household	11.5	3.81	1.784	0.0091
ALL/Model R²	5.6		0.245	

Overall, based on model R square statistics (Nagelkereke) these models explain between 22 and 28% of the variance in our dependent variable wealthy/not wealthy and in each of the four analyses the absence of dependent children in the household was among the most powerful predictors of wealth. In comparison with households with children, those without children were between 4.2 and 8.2 times more likely to be wealthy, once other predictors are included in our model.

This table shows that, for example, in combining the 1970-72 Family Expenditure Survey samples and the 1971 Census, the following was estimated as the number of exclusive wealthy households in each tract: 3.1% of high social class households (with head of household in social class I or II) + 1.5% of owner-occupied households + 4.3% of households with no dependent children + 2.2% of households where the head of household was in work + 1.6% of households with seven or more rooms + 2.9% of households with two or more cars.

Reasons for not using the census method

Producing estimates of the geographical distribution of the exclusive wealthy for small areas at different points in time proved to be one of the most difficult technical challenges of this work. We have theoretical models of what it means to be exclusively wealthy that have been developed over decades, and can produce practical models that estimate the proportion of people who have wealth to such a degree from the surveys of income and expenditure, as described above. However, the nature of the surveys, and more importantly of the census, means that we cannot estimate the geography of the exclusive wealthy in the same manner as we do for the poor.

The estimates of exclusive wealthy produced by the alternative method highlighted the inability of questions asked in the censuses to distinguish 'wealthy' households or people, relative to their very powerful ability to pick out poor people and households. The very low weightings of the census variables (as listed in Table A4) mean that they are extremely sensitive to local variation in what indicates wealth. For example, while it would be fair to assume that a fairly large proportion of households with seven or more rooms in Kensington and Chelsea were wealthy in 1980, the proportion of houses with the same number of rooms in rural Norfolk that were wealthy was probably considerably lower. However, the model for 1980 estimates that in every tract, 1.6% of households with seven or more rooms would be exclusive wealthy. This type of local variation may well also affect the breadline poverty method (see the section on 'Locally sensitive poverty measures', Chapter 7, page 48) but the weightings in the wealth equations are so low that the effect is likely to be dramatic.

Histograms for the 1980 exclusive wealthy measures calculated using both methods are charted in Figure A1. This shows the estimates using the census (the green line) to be concentrated within a very small range of values, from around 4-9%, and following a symmetrical distribution. The estimates using the asset wealthy methodology conform much more to what we would expect of this measure: a reasonably large proportion of tracts have no exclusive wealthy households (whereas the census method found some in

Figure A1: Histograms of 1980 exclusive wealthy percentages across all tracts using both methods

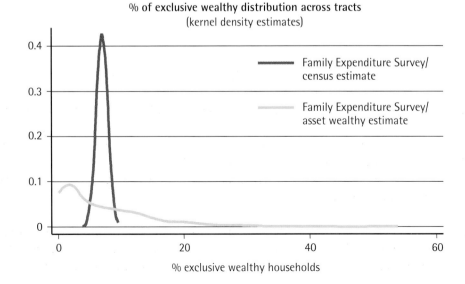

% of exclusive wealthy distribution across tracts
(kernel density estimates)

Family Expenditure Survey/
census estimate

Family Expenditure Survey/
asset wealthy estimate

% exclusive wealthy households

every tract); most tracts have a fairly low proportion of exclusive wealthy households; the distribution is highly positively skewed – the distribution tails off gradually, with just a very few tracts having a high proportion of exclusive wealthy households. The symmetrical distribution found by the census method is really very unlikely, as is the very low highest value of 9%. We would expect the very wealthiest tracts in the country to have many more exclusive wealthy households than just 9%.

The graph in Figure A2 shows the different wealth estimates, including the estimated exclusive wealthy proportion using the census method. As stated above, the upper set of estimates (median method) were used to calibrate the asset wealthy method to produce small area estimates of exclusive wealth.

Figure A2: The wealth measures, including exclusive wealthy, from the alternative (Family Expenditure Survey/census) method

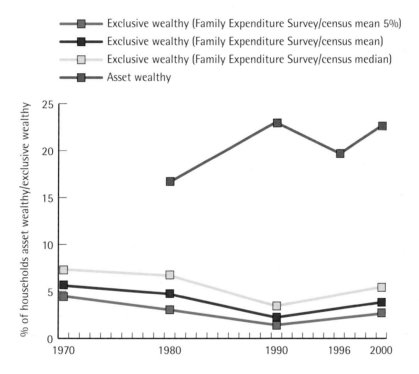

Wealth indices: validation

Share ownership 1990

Since no other small area estimates of wealth or wealthy populations are available, and our measures are novel, it would seem prudent to attempt to validate our measures to the extent possible. One dataset available to us that could be considered to reflect wealth contains details of share ownership in 1990. This dataset includes information on the number of people holding shares in private companies, and the number holding shares in privatised utilities, along with the values of shares held. These data were available for 1991 Census wards, and could therefore be aggregated to tracts and compared with the asset and exclusive wealthy measures.

For each tract, we calculated the proportion of households with a shareholder (assuming that few households would have more than one shareholder), and also the total value of private company shares owned. We used only private shares and shareholders, rather than privatised utility shares, for these analyses. This is because the privatised utility shares were widely advertised, and sold in such a way as to be highly accessible to many people. This is especially the case given the vintage of these data, and the widespread selling-off of state-run industries and services around that time. Shares in private companies would, however, have continued to be held by more 'traditional' investors in stocks and shares, who might be thought of as wealthy. The associations between these variables and the percentage of households classified as asset or exclusive wealthy in 1990 are illustrated in the charts in Figure A3.

The correlation coefficient for the association between asset wealthy and the proportion of households holding shares was 0.71, and that for the association between asset wealthy and total shareholdings value was 0.50. The equivalent correlation coefficients for the exclusive wealthy measure were 0.46 and 0.45 respectively.

Figure A3: Associations between asset and exclusive wealthy and the % of households owning shares in private companies, and total shareholdings value, by tract

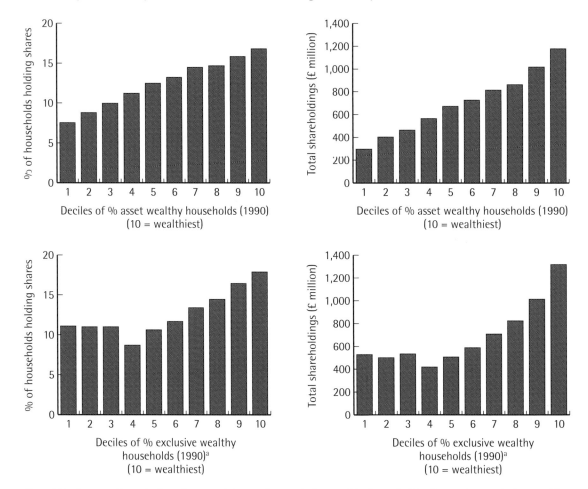

Note: [a] The bottom three deciles of tracts with regard to exclusive wealthy households all contain 0 exclusive wealthy households.

The charts and correlation coefficients demonstrate a strong association between the wealth measures and the share ownership measures, providing some degree of reassurance that our wealth measures are valid. This is particularly the case for the association between the percentage of households classified as asset wealthy and the percentage of households owning shares, which would make sense. The associations with total value of shareholdings are influenced by several outliers, those tracts where extremely high values of shares are owned.

Luxury car ownership 1999

Another dataset available is that collated by Experian on car ownership by manufacturer. These data were available for postcode sectors for 1999, and these were aggregated to tracts via a postcode to enumeration district look up table.[13] Car marques classified as 'luxury' cars for the purposes of this analysis were Alfa Romeo, Audi, Bentley, BMW, Ferrari, Jaguar, Lexus and Mercedes Benz, and for each tract the proportion of cars falling into these marques was calculated. We then measured the association between our wealthy households' measures for 1999 and this luxury car proportion in a similar way to the shares analysis above.

The charts presented in Figure A4 demonstrate a moderate degree of association between luxury car ownership and asset and exclusive wealthy. The correlation coefficients for the measures across all tracts are 0.38 for asset wealthy and 0.53 for exclusive wealthy. Again, there are few 'outlier' tracts with very high levels of luxury car ownership.

Figure A4: Associations between asset and exclusive wealthy and luxury car share, by tract

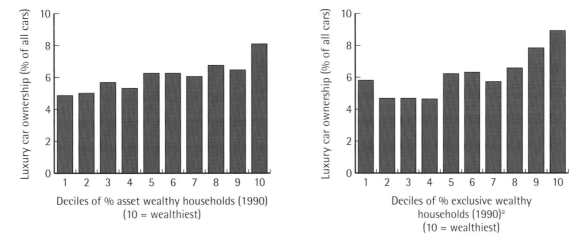

Note: [a] The bottom three deciles of tracts with regard to exclusive wealthy households all contain 0 exclusive wealthy households.

Spatial concentration methods

The analysis of the spatial concentration of poverty and wealth presented in the section on 'Spatial clustering' (Chapter 6, page 36) and Chapter 8 uses the freely available spatial analysis software package GeoDa.[14] In order to calculate both global Moran's I statistics and Local Indicators of Spatial Association (LISA) for the poverty and wealth datasets, the software first had to be used to construct a set of 'spatial weights' for the tracts. These spatial weights simply define how each tract is spatially related to all other tracts, and can be calculated in a variety of ways. These analyses used the simplest method of 'first order contiguity weights', meaning that each tract was associated with all of its immediate neighbours (those tracts sharing a boundary).

---

[13] A number of postcode sectors did not match to enumeration districts, and cars in these sectors were excluded. Since these missing values were geographically clustered, they resulted in no car data for 18 of the 1,282 tracts; this error is unlikely to substantially affect findings.

[14] GeoDa can be obtained from the Spatial Analysis Laboratory (SAL) at the University of Illinois, Urbana-Champaign (http://sal.uiuc.edu/).

For each variable, for example, the percentage of households classified as breadline poor, GeoDa was then used to calculate (a) the global Moran's I statistic and (b) LISA statistics for each tract. A randomised simulation procedure is used to estimate the statistical significance of these statistics, and for each type an additional 999 simulations were run to produce what should be relatively robust results.

The concept of statistical significance with LISA statistics such as those presented here is slightly complex, since it falls foul of the 'multiple tests' problem. For each measure, for each tract, a LISA statistic and corresponding p-value are calculated. If the p-value is less than 0.05 (in this case), the indicator (high cluster, low cluster, high spatial outlier or low spatial outlier) is mapped; if the p-value is more than 0.05, it is not ('little local spatial autocorrelation' on the maps). Since each map includes 1,282 of these tests, and each test is saying 'is the probability that this result could be due to chance less than 1 in 20 (0.05)', we are likely to say that some LISA statistics are significant due to chance alone. However, adjustments for this multiple testing problem can be overly conservative. More importantly, we are interested in the overall geographical patterns produced by this analysis, rather than the result for a single tract. Given that the analyses are presented here as exploratory, and confirmatory with regard to the other maps and analyses presented in the report, this issue is not likely to have any considerable effect on our findings or conclusions.

Higher Education participation

In the section on 'Education' (Chapter 8, page 69), we describe the changes in Higher Education (HE) participation rates derived from HE Funding Council for England (HEFCE) data. A 2005 HEFCE report (Corver, 2005) uses a similar analysis, and comes up with similar results, although it uses a different spatial unit and has an annual time series rather than just two points to compare. The HEFCE analysis of participation rates by parliamentary constituency shown in Figure A5 indicates that the quintile with the highest overall participation rates saw the largest absolute increases across the six years. This is slightly different to our findings (see the section on 'Education', as above, and Figure 15), as we found similar absolute increases for the top deciles to the bottom deciles.

Figure A5: Results of HEFCE analysis of HE young participation rates: absolute change since 1994

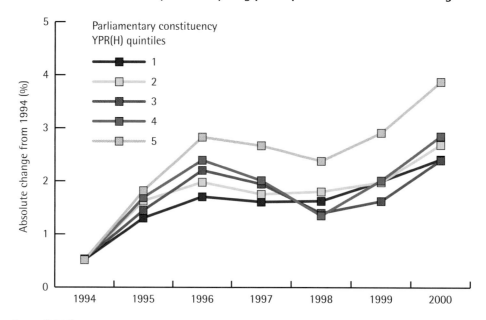

Source: Corver (2005)

In agreement with our results, Figure A6 suggests that the greatest proportional rise was among those areas in the lowest quintile.

Figure A6: Results of HEFCE analysis of HE young participation rates: relative change since 1994

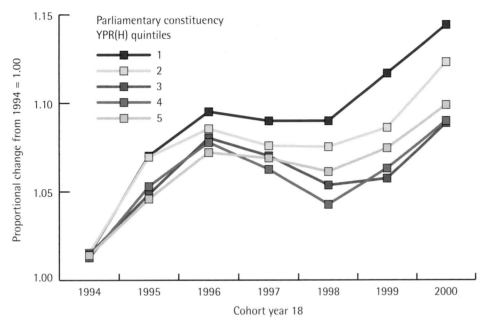

Source: Corver (2005)

Appendix 2: Additional maps

Map A1: Change in breadline poverty rates over time

1970 to 1980

1980 to 1990

1990 to 2000

Breadline poor % point change

<-10
-10 to -5
-5 to 0
0 to +5
+5 to +10
+10 to +15
>+15

Maps illustrate the absolute change in percentage of households classified as breadline poor over the decade indicated.

Map A2: Change in core poverty rates over time

1970 to 1980

1980 to 1990

1990 to 2000

Core poor % change

<-15
-15 to -10
-10 to -5
-5 to 0
0 to +5
+5 to +10
>+10

Maps illustrate the absolute change in percentage of households classified as core poor over the decade indicated.

Map A3: Change in asset wealthy % over time

1980 to 1990

1990 to 1996

1996 to 2000

Asset wealthy % point change

<-20
-20 to -10
-10 to 0
0 to +10
+10 to +20
>+20

Maps illustrate the absolute change in percentage of households classified as asset wealthy during the period indicated.

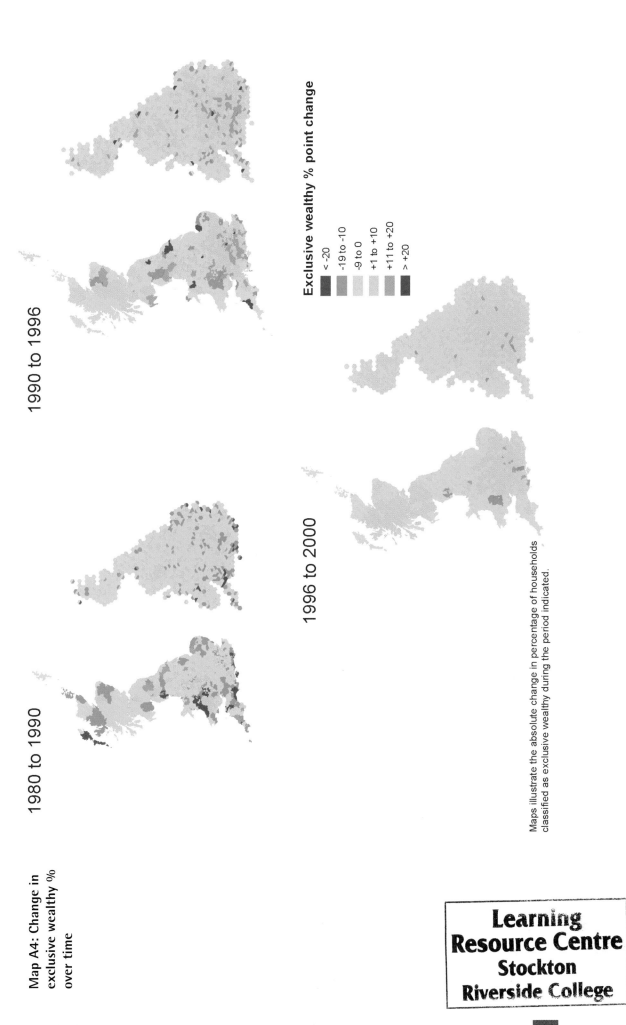

Map A4: Change in exclusive wealthy % over time

1980 to 1990

1990 to 1996

1996 to 2000

Exclusive wealthy % point change

< -20
-19 to -10
-9 to 0
+1 to +10
+11 to +20
> +20

Maps illustrate the absolute change in percentage of households classified as exclusive wealthy during the period indicated.